Book Reviews

"WILL YOU TAKE THIS BABY? *is the true story of Mary Jones and her experiences as a foster mother in the Washington State foster care system. Mary chronicles her journey of caring for infants in the system, and her advocacy for critical care babies. Mary's story is one of love, dedication, and determination. She provides a foster home for infants who are medically fragile and at risk of being placed in a nursing home or other institutions. Mary advocates for these infants, and works to ensure that they receive the best possible care. This book is a heart-warming and inspiring story of one woman's dedication to making a difference in the lives of the infants in her care. It is a must-read for anyone interested in foster care, advocacy, or making a difference in the lives of others."*

— **Junayd Coombes, Reprospace Editorial Book Reviews™**

"This groundbreaking book written by a foster mom about her journey of caring for infants in the Washington State Foster Care System, and her advocacy for critical care babies is an inspirational and heart-wrenching account of one woman's experience as a foster mom to infants in the state's foster care system. Mary Jones provides a rare, intimate look into the challenges and rewards of caring for some of the most vulnerable children in our society. She chronicles her journey as a foster mom with honesty and courage, and shares her deep commitment to advocating for the needs of these special babies. This book is a must-read for anyone who cares about children, and is a powerful reminder of the importance of love and nurturing in the lives of all children."

— **Neriah Grey, Reprospace Editorial Book Reviews™**

A FOSTER MOTHER'S JOURNEY

CARING AND FIGHTING FOR THE MOST FRAGILE INFANTS

Mary, will you take this baby?

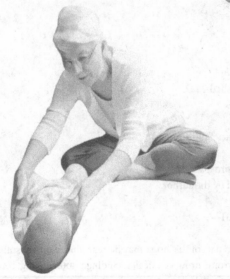

MARY STILLSON JONES

Will You Take This Baby?
Second edition, published 2022.
By Mary Stillson Jones

Copyright © 2022, Mary Stillson Jones

Interior Layout by Reprospace
Cover image provided by the author.

ISBN: 978-1-952685-51-4

Published by Kitsap Publishing
Poulsbo, WA 98370
www.KitsapPublishing.com
Published and printed in the United States of America

Prologue

"One hundred years from now, it will not matter what kind of house I lived in, how much money I had, nor what my clothes looked like, but the world may be a little bit better because I was important in the life of a child."

—Author Unknown

I felt compelled to write this book, just as I was compelled to take each baby. Tiny, helpless, and struggling to survive, Jose had a hole in his heart, Hannah was in a detox center for infants, Claire needed testing for HIV, and Mathew had half a heart. They touched my life so profoundly. How could I *not* feel compelled to take each one? I felt our experiences warranted being shared so others could gain insight into the world of foster care, what giving back is all about, and seeing beyond ourselves.

I often questioned my ability to care for the most fragile infants because I was *just a Mom*. I didn't realize at the time just a Mom was what each one needed most, a force to be reckoned with.

I did whatever it took to get the best for the children who had the least.

Loving my babies was by far the driving force they needed to feel to survive. I was humbled by their presence, in admiration of their strength, and honored to have had them in my life.

For every baby, I've held in my arms and continue to hold in my heart.

Mary L. Jones

PART I

WHO I AM

"To know who I am is to understand where I find my joy."
—**Mary Stillson Jones**

I grew up in Ontario, Canada, the third of four children. My dad was an engineer, and my mom was a stay-at-home mom. We had everything we needed or wanted. We knew we were loved, and life was good.

Our home was on the bank of the St. Lawrence River. Nearby deserted islands provided many adventures, countless picnics, and hours of fun. Our only close neighbor was Grandma and Grandpa. As kids, if Mom were baking, as she did most every day, we'd hang over the fence bordering Grandpa's farm, with an extra-large cookie or doughnut made just for him when he passed by on the tractor.

During the summer months, we couldn't get in enough swimming. Daddy would stand in the water at the end of the dock, and whether he was ready or not, we'd run and yell, "Catch me, Daddy." And he always did.

When summer turned into winter and the ice formed, we skated every day. All four of us kids loved to lie spread-eagle on the frozen river with our noses pressed to the ice looking down into the deep cracks. It was scary, but that was the fun of it, and of course, Mom and Dad were always arm's length away.

Come December, holiday time was resplendent with copious decorations, and on Christmas morning, the floor was all but covered with presents, including a beautiful new toboggan. Santa always seemed to know the one from the previous year was worn out from four kids, eight rosy cheeks, and mountains of snow well into May some years. Those were special times, and looking back, I thought that was how all children grew up.

When I turned eight we moved to a small town not far away. For the first time in my life we had close neighbors with lots of children to play with. We were outside more than inside, jumping rope, playing hopscotch, high jump, or marbles until calluses formed on our fingers.

The community playground became our second home, a gathering place for all the neighborhood kids. As we got older, out came balls and bats, we played until dark all summer long. Bicycles took us on countless rides down country lanes, each of us carrying a packed lunch thanks to Mom as we set off. Those were different times. They were the best of time.

Dad worked for DuPont and the company had its own private beach. Mom often spent all morning packing one of her special picnics, then we'd head on over. We swam and played all afternoon, then Dad joined us after work for a picnic dinner. As darkness set in he'd build a big fire down by the water and several families would gather round, talking, laughing, roasting marshmallows and watching the flickering bonfire light up the night sky. I can picture it in my mind's eye to this very day.

My brothers became obsessed with go-carts. Every boy in the neighborhood had one, hand-made, painted, and accessorized. Of course each claimed theirs would go the fastest. Skinned knees, sprained wrists and ankles didn't slow them down. Every little girl in town who had a doll buggy had to be very vigilant because their wheels were disappearing at an alarming rate and showing up on go-carts.

There were several babies on my court...boy did I like those babies! I was ten and would often run home from school just to walk one of them around the neighborhood. Their moms thought it was great. It gave them time to tidy the house, prepare dinner, or just put their feet up for an hour or so. I became the neighborhood baby sitter.

I attended parochial school for eight years. The nuns wore long dresses called a *habit* that swished when they walked past. It was formal, strict schooling, and much was expected of us. I recall getting in trouble twice. Once for not speaking loud enough, and once when Sister Mary Theresa intercepted a note from a boy to me in seventh grade. I was admonished and told not to encourage "such nonsense", but was never privy to what the note said!

High school came next. That was a big adjustment. No more uniforms, male teachers, dances, and most of each day was spent changing classrooms, or so it seemed. I never had to do that before.

I had no idea what I wanted to do with my life, but I knew for sure what I didn't want to do...sit behind a desk or work in a bank, what most of my classmates aspired to at the time.

The day President Kennedy was killed was the day I decided on my future. I was in class when his assassination was announced over the loud speaker. Stillness filled the air, and as the hours passed, sadness touched the world unlike anything I'd ever witnessed before. That day I made my decision; I was going to join the United States Navy. My podunk little town wasn't enough for me anymore. I wanted to see the world that sadness brought to its knees.

Over the next four years my family watched and listened, wondering if I was serious, or if I'd change my mind. They had always let us kids make our own decisions, encouraged us, at the same time assuring us we could always go back to them for input. They laid a full tuition paid university option on the table. When that didn't dissuade me, they gave me their blessing. I was steadfast in my decision, and when graduation time came it was clear to all I would soon be wearing a military uniform, in another country, at war in Vietnam. I wanted adventure, and I wanted to make a difference. I wanted to help.

It took nearly a year to sort through all the red tape because I wasn't a U.S. citizen. It was worth the wait, culminating with me sitting before the American Consulate General, in Montreal, for the final paper signing. Just the placard on his office door was intimidating enough. I was astonished at the size of his desk. To this day I often wonder where I found the nerve to do some of the things I did back then. A month later Mom and Dad were waving goodbye as my bus drove out of sight. I was headed for Bainbridge Maryland, Navy Boot Camp for women.

In retrospect, boot camp should be a prerequisite for adulthood. I never dreamed I could walk with my shoulders back so far, nor my head held so high. Aside from deportment, we had classes throughout the day in military training, aircraft, and weaponry, as well as marching, marching, and more marching!

I couldn't believe I had to send all my civilian clothes home. Whatever I felt like wearing was replaced with the uniform of the day. I learned new vocabulary too; the bathroom was now the *head*, and my purse was replaced with a *ditty bag*. From never having to make my bed at home, now I had to lie underneath it and make sure the sheets were perfectly flat between the springs. It was, "Yes Ma'am, No Ma'am," all day long.

Once a week we had to send a *duty letter* home to allay any of our parent's anxieties. We were encouraged to tell them how we were getting along. Several of mine were very brief and to the point. They simply said, "Get me out of here."

Remember I said my parents were encouraging and reassuring? They were also of the belief that one must live with the consequences of their choices in order to learn, grow, and succeed in life. I learned to live with mine, and looking back I'm thankful and grateful I found the strength to see them through.

Graduation day arrived. Mom and Dad flew in for the ceremonies, and as I passed in review I could see the pride on their faces. Our family had a combined military service of seventy-two years, including two world wars. I was honored to be added to the role call as the first woman in the bunch.

While in the service I married, and when I finished my enlistment, I joined my military husband on duty at the American Embassy in London, England.

I was always looking for adventure and England had a colorful history. As my plane made its final approach into Heathrow Airport late that January night, I remember the look of intrigue and mystery from the air surrounding the lampposts with their yellow lights cloaked in shrouds of fog and mist. Jack the Ripper came to mind right away although it was 1971.

For the next year and a half, any free time we had we traveled throughout Europe. We visited every tourist attraction in the United Kingdom, and made ourselves dizzy exploring countless castles and museums. That's what people do whilst in England, but it all changed with a visit to my doctor. "You're pregnant!"

We were thrilled. Having never been a very patient person, waiting nine months for a baby was more than a little difficult.

Once the shock wore off, I busied myself with the preparations; baby furniture, buggies, and clothes, then sat back and waited, and waited…I thought, if Rome was built in a day, why did having a baby take nine whole months!!

The day Tara Dawn Jones was placed in my arms, I felt as if I was eye to eye with the eighth wonder of the world. I was a MOM, and couldn't wait to begin this new and exciting chapter of my life.

Five days later we took Tara home, and one day later I wasn't seeing her as the eighth wonder of the world anymore, but rather someone to be stamped *return to sender!*

If you've ever had a child with colic you'll understand my saying that. From day one she suffered with it so severely she would turn blue, and screamed for hours on end every day. Colic is severe abdominal pain caused by intestinal gas in infants.

There was no way I'd consider having more babies until her pediatrician prescribed a mild sedative so Donald and I could finally get some sleep. That said, four months later the colic subsided and our little Miss became the joy of our life. More babies was a definite possibility.

Things don't always turn out as planned though. Her first two years were plagued with a myriad of medical issues. She began having grand mal seizures, and at one point doctors feared she had leukemia. Thankfully she did not, but we had reservations about having more children. Donald's twin sister gave birth to a son with a serious, lifelong disorder. It was unclear why, or if a twin could pass it on. We were not prepared to take the risk and made the decision not to have any more children.

As Tara grew stronger and healthier, my desire for another child came back. I desperately wanted another baby. At thirty two that was considered old to start again, so I tried to put it out of my mind.

We were still a military family, now stationed in Connecticut, when television ran an appeal for foster parents. I remember thinking we could have many babies. Donald liked the idea, and nine months later, yes, nine months, a baby boy was delivered to our front door. That was only the start.

As you turn the pages of this book, you will go back with me on my journey of a lifetime. Thirty-one years of heartbreak and sorrow. Thirty-one years of holding miracles in my arms. Thirty-one years of loving unconditionally.

PART II

MY BABIES

Sam

It all started with Baby Sam. He was two months old, and along with two siblings were removed from their birth mother for severe neglect. His brother and sister were together in another foster home. Sam had been left on his own day after day with only a blanket and a bottle propped against his cheek. When he came to us he didn't respond to human touch nor could he smile.

Children who experience neglect often fare much worse than children of abuse because they have little to no human contact. Doctors have told me the first few months of life are critical in a child's development. It's when they bond and form attachments. The window of opportunity to accomplish this is small, and left too long can result in serious lifelong repercussions.

After nine months of classes and home studies, reality sank in. It had been ten years since we had a baby in the house so there was much to get reacquainted with, and so many rules and regulations that hadn't come with our

9

daughter. But Sam settled in nicely and believe me when I say how thankful I was that he didn't have colic!

The back of his head was flat and he didn't respond appropriately to his environment, indicative of neglect. He gulped down his formula but didn't interact at all. It would take time and lots of love and attention to gain his trust.

It wasn't long before we were so enamored of him we'd have to remind ourselves that the day would come when we'd have to let him go, either back to his birth mother or be placed up for adoption. In Connecticut at that time, foster parents could not adopt their foster children.

When he turned eleven months old, the state formulated a plan to see if he could safely be returned to his mother. With classes, support and extensive help, she needed to prove she was better able to parent her son. Over a period of several weeks, the social worker was to pick him up from our house in the morning, and he'd spend the day with his Mom, then be returned to us each evening. Though it was hard, we got him ready for his first visit and kissed him goodbye.

Two hours later his social worker called to say he was returning with Sam. His birth mother requested he be placed up for adoption. They never saw each other again.

We went about our lives enjoying every minute with Sam knowing it wouldn't be long before someone wanting a son would fall in love with him.

Instead, to our surprise, a few weeks later the Department of Social and Health Services asked if we'd like to adopt Sam. We couldn't say *yes* fast enough. The rules were changing in favor of the child.

Not wanting Tara to feel left out, we asked her to pick his new name, wheels were set in motion, and in May 1983, *now Jonathan*, became our son will all the pomp and ceremony befitting the occasion. He was our first foster baby and I often joke with him that he stayed the longest, thirty-five years and counting. A high percentage of foster parents now adopt at least one of their foster children. It was a good change.

In the days ahead a newborn baby needed temporary placement, she was already free for adoption, and a family was cleared to take her, but last minute details required a short stay in foster care with us. My-oh-my, that was eye opening. Two babies! All those bottles and diaper changes in the wee hours of the night, but we adjusted and she soon fit right in. A month later she left with her new forever family. My foot was firmly in the door of foster parenting. I was in my element and wanted more.

I soon learned that while I was growing up safe and sound, many children were not. Over the years I have witnessed many disturbing cases. I've dealt with baby after baby suffering through withdrawals from drugs and the effects of alcohol. In the system, it's not unusual for a Mom to have three or more children taken away, yet go on to give birth to more. They too, more often than not, taken away as well.

Because I'd dealt with my daughter's medical issues, and my nephew's, I was somewhat at ease in a crisis, so perhaps it wasn't out of left field that I began taking sicker and sicker babies, medically fragile, and critical care infants. The more experience I got, the more at ease I became.

I was so excited when each one arrived, as if they were my own. Some were only hours old when I picked them up at the hospital. Some I got to know over weeks, even months, while still in the hospital waiting to be well enough for me to take home. Hospital staff trained me to take care of their special needs. That included giving injections. I practiced on apples and oranges for days until I felt confident enough to give a baby his next shot. I must have appeared over-confident because the attending nurse looked at me with a smile and said, "It's quite different when you're holding a *real* tiny leg." She was right of course, but I prided myself for learning how and not being afraid.

When fragile babies came into my care it was not uncommon to see health vans dropping off huge oxygen tanks and monitors, nor to see fire trucks and aid vehicles in my driveway. Neighbors got used to it.

I made sure to welcome each one with balloons and fanfare just as anyone would do for their own children. I tried to make everything normal for them. Written documentations, photographs, and videos were very important to send with the babies when they left so they could look back in years to come and know they were loved, valued, and wanted.

With the arrival of each new baby, it was commonplace to be out and about with a couple of monitors, oxygen tank, feeding tubes, and diaper bag all in tow. My babies needed care, but they also needed socialization and a smile on their face. People started calling me "The Baby Lady."

It's said it takes a village to raise a child. For my babies it couldn't have been truer. Without the support, encouragement and caring I got from my community, I couldn't have walked the walk.

People have asked me many questions over the years. The one I got most was, "How can you keep them so long, love them, and then let them go?" It was always easy to answer. "Now they'll have a Mommy and Daddy of their own, life's greatest gift." It's all I ever wanted for them. Though I missed them dearly, I was very happy for them.

My babies stayed varying lengths of time, some for a few hours, a day or two, and some for a few years. The most common was about eighteen months. It didn't matter how long, they brought joy into my life and I learned so much from each one. They showed me what I was capable of, and I drew

12

strength from their strength. Some came from horrendous circumstances, reminding me of the many blessings in my own life.

For a while I did emergency placements as well as regular foster care. I had two nurseries set up and ready to use at any time. On occasion police officers dropped off babies in the middle of the night. Some from domestic violence situations, some from the back seat of parked cars behind taverns. On one such night I recall the officer handing me a diaper bag suggesting I be very careful putting my hand in for fear of jabbing myself on a needle. Thereafter I always emptied diaper bags on the porch.

I'm often asked where the babies are now, how they are doing, and if I keep in touch. I do with some, always mindful of the new parents' privacy. Some want to keep a connection, others don't, and that's okay, I understand. Sometimes a phone call, or a card with a photo lights up my very soul.

I wanted adventure and a chance to make a difference in the world. I did both, and now I realize they were one and the same, at different times in my life.

Mathew

The doors of the emergency room flew open. I had four month old Mathew in my arms. When the nurse looked up, my face alone told her I needed help fast. She ran over, took him from my arms as another nurse hovered around trying to get me to sit down.

"We need information", she said. "You have to calm yourself. Your baby is in good hands." I couldn't calm myself, I knew he could go into cardiac arrest at any time.

It sounded like a normal call from the placement desk. A baby boy with heart issues needed a home. He was in Children's Hospital waiting to be released. Would I consider taking him? That afternoon I was on my way to meet Mathew. As I entered the parking garage I remember thinking I'd been there so often I should have my own spot by now.

I was always saddened on entering the hospital. The first thing you notice are children in wheelchairs, babies in specialized strollers, and young kids walking with IV's attached to them, or trailing behind. Then there were the faces of parents, tired, worn out, and frightened. I had to remind myself what I couldn't see were the many success stories. Children on the road to recovery, feeling better every day. Smiles returning, and futures looking brighter and brighter.

As I entered Mathew's room, two nurses turned to greet me. Beside them lay the sickest baby I'd ever seen. He looked so tiny and helpless in a room filled with machines. He was asleep, oblivious to the scary scene that surrounded him. To be truthful, I didn't know if I should turn and run. It must have showed on my face because one of the nurses put her arm around me and assured me he was resting comfortably. I reached over and touched his tiny hand noticing how blue he looked. I wanted to pick him up but I was terrified, not of him, but of all the equipment hooked up to his tiny body. Hospital staff took me into an adjacent room where we sat around a table and Mathew's condition was explained. His diagnosis was Hypoplastic Left Heart Syndrome. He was a critical care cardiac baby. The left side of his heart was underdeveloped, a rare uncorrectable birth defect. He'd already gone through open heart surgery right after birth called the Norwood Procedure. Now the right side of his heart was struggling to keep him alive. A series of three open heart procedures had proven to benefit babies like Mathew. Together they would stabilize his heart until the right side showed signs of failure, at which time he'd be placed on a list for a transplant. Some babies would survive all three, some would not. The cardiac surgeon made sure I understood a new heart was inevitable, but no one could say when with any certainty.

I had to decide whether I could take Mathew home and care for him. I roamed around the hospital for hours, watching, listening, and thinking. In the end my decision was easy. Would I walk away from my own baby because he had a birth defect, or would I love him, learn to care for him, and take him home? It was decided.

After countless trips back and forth to the hospital, sleeping on a chair-bed beside him many nights, and undergoing extensive training unlike any I'd had before, Mathew and I were ready. We were going home. For three months I felt safe with him in the hospital setting. Now his life was in my hands.

As we packed up to leave, two nurse practitioners were giving me last minute instructions when I asked point blank if the hospital was sending Mathew home with me for palliative care. They hadn't expected my question and were noticeably caught off guard. I told them I could only deal with what I knew, and asked them to please be honest. They looked at each other, then told me there were no certainties. They couldn't say further because they didn't know.

Leaving the hospital, I was scared to death something would happen in city traffic and I'd have nowhere to pull over to summon help. I requested the state provide an aid to make the trip home with us, but it was denied. I put my fears on hold, focused on my responsibilities, and found the *stuff* inside me that gave me strength. I went back to my military training.

Once home, I watched for signs of cardiac arrest and congestive heart failure. Four times during the day I monitored oxygen levels that sometimes dropped dangerously low. I gave him continuous feeds through an internal feeding pump, and drew up, at one point, twenty three doses of medication throughout the day, all administered through yet another tube in his stomach. I learned how each one worked, what to watch for, and how to react if something went wrong. I gave him two injections, and recorded his vital signs twice daily. I was trained to do oral feeding therapy because all his nourishment was administered through a tube, and physical as well as therapeutic exercises. Mathew was dependent on me. I could not fail him. His oxygen levels hovered in the sixties, normal being ninety to one hundred. If it went lower for any length of time, I was to call 911. A huge oxygen tank sat in the corner of the family room, and hundreds of feet of tubing wound its way throughout my house, up the stairs into the night nursery. At bath time I attached the tubing to the side of the shower curtain with clothes pins. I slept two feet away from his crib, and the whir of his feeding pump lulled us both to sleep. I went to bed at the same time setting three alarms to ensure I'd not miss giving him meds during the night. His care was great, but he was greater. I loved him.

On more than one occasion I had to call 911, most often due to a drop in oxygen. We made numerous trips to my local hospital when I had any concerns. They made the decision if he was stable enough for me to transport to Children's Hospital by car, or if an ambulance or medevac was necessary. Before long ambulance drivers knew us by our first names.

Prior to leaving the hospital I asked the social worker for a health and safety plan should I become ill and not be able to care for Mathew. Normally, if a foster mom is sick, another foster mom will step in and help. His condition was tenuous, and no one else was trained to take on the enormous responsibility. I needed a plan but it was not forthcoming.

Over the next several months I pressed for one but it never materialized. Then one evening I fell to the floor and had to call the paramedics for myself. Thinking I'd had a stroke, they prepared to transport me to the hospital. I told them I wasn't going anywhere until Mathew was taken care of. I explained they had no choice but to call a second ambulance to take him to Children's Hospital. My local ER was not equipped to deal with his many needs, they agreed. It was seven p.m. before we were both in an ambulance. Mine left first.

Around midnight I was discharged home and called Children's Hospital to check on Mathew, he wasn't there. He had not been admitted. They checked the emergency room, he wasn't there either. By now it was one a.m. and I was frantic. I couldn't find a critical care, cardiac infant, who the state entrusted to my care, who by now missed many meds, and at any time his feeding pump would alarm indicating he was out of food. Frantic hardly describes how I felt. I called the on-duty social worker and explained my situation. While I paced the floor, she did some checking, and thirty minutes later Mathew was located at my local hospital awaiting a life support ambulance to transport him to Children's Hospital. He had been there six hours. Instead, I asked he be returned to me. I could take care of him.

17

Thankfully I did not have a stroke, and days later I went looking for answers as to why he was not transported as arranged. The answer was because there was never a health and safety plan in place as I requested so many times, and, no one knew what to do with him. Children's Hospital misunderstood the circumstances and declined to take him. A police officer and on-call social worker were called to my home. I had no idea this was happening because my ambulance left first. I was later told Mathew lay in his ambulance for two hours, in my driveway, while police and state officials discussed what to do, all because no one listened to me.

Within days our lives returned to our new normal. I was feeling much better and Mathew was doing well. With renewed determination, I set about making sure this would never happen again. It was not as simple as making a few phone calls or writing letters. It took almost two years, many meetings, collaborations, and contacting the right people. There had never been policy in place addressing the needs of fragile babies in foster care. That would soon change. When I see something that is so wrong, I must do whatever it takes to make it so right. Policy now stands.

There was never a dull moment with Mathew in my life. I took him for a routine check-up one day and the doctor told me she was nervous just having him in her office. That didn't bode well with me considering I was taking him home!

Another time I had to reassure an ambulance paramedic that Mathew would be just fine en route to the hospital. That's not to say I didn't have moments when I was scared beyond belief myself.

Giving him his shot one evening something didn't feel right. Mathew gave no indication that anything was wrong. I took the needle over to a brighter light and was shocked to see it was bent in half. I had no way of knowing how much medicine went into his leg, or if some ran down the side. I made a quick call to the cardiologist who explained I more than likely hit scar tissue when I put the needle in from repeated shots over the months. I thought, couldn't someone have covered that possibility when I was being trained! I was instructed to draw up half a dose and watch him closely for the next six hours.

Sleep evaded me that night. Instead, I lay there crying, the bed shaking beneath me. If I made one mistake, just one small mistake, I knew Mathew could die.

A few weeks later we were again in my local emergency room. His feeding tube came out, and since it was inserted past the stomach into the duodenum, medical personnel had to put it back in. I had been warned this could happen, to not be alarmed, go to the hospital. Having just returned from a routine check-up with his pediatrician, I had all the paperwork with me. Once there, they decided to send him to Seattle's Children Hospital via ambulance. Several medications were due, as well as an injection before he was to leave. I gave the nurse all his charts listing each medicine and dose. She was preparing to give him his shot when I told her it looked like too much. She explained they used different needles so it *just looked like* too much. I didn't question her further, she was a nurse, we were in an emergency room, so it must be right. *It was not.*

Nothing happened until an hour later. The doctor was replacing his feeding tube when four other doctors burst in to tell us a nurse called believing she gave Mathew *ten times* the prescribed dose, *in the needle I queried.*

His doctors were uncertain how he would respond, they could only wait and watch. He was admitted and went into a semi-comatose state for the next five days. It could have killed him. Fortunately he suffered no lasting effects. Had the nurse not owned up to her mistake, and something tragic happened, the finger would have been pointed squarely at me.

19

I was never privy to actions resulting from what transpired that day. However, weeks later, on another harried trip to the emergency room, the same nurse was on duty. She identified herself and left the room.

Today as I put my pen to paper and remember my days with Mathew, my heart smiles. I still have a binder that holds all his charts. At the end of each day I'd often write a note. On October 23, 2009, my entry read, "I am thankful for my day with Mathew. For his smile, his eyes, his giggle, and his tiny fingers. I am humbled by his presence. I have no doubt he is an angle walking in my life."

In caring for him I learned that a very small person can teach very big lessons, about life, death, and unconditional love; how to live in the moment, and how to put someone else first.

When he turned eight months old, his team of cardiologists scheduled his second open heart surgery, a procedure called the Glynn, to redirect the flow of blood through his heart. He had put on weight, was much stronger than he was for his first surgery, and in general, he was doing well. I was told he'd likely be out of the hospital within a week. The state arranged for me to stay at a nearby hotel so I could be there for him.

The day of surgery I was panicked. I paced the halls, I ate, I paced some more. Then word came, he was in ICU. I could breath normally again.

That said, I wasn't prepared for the moment I saw him. He lay with arms outstretched, a large dressing covering most of his stomach, and a mass of staples lined the incision down the center of his chest. The all too familiar machines were back beeping and blinking. Wires, tubes, and nurses surrounded his tiny limp body. I covered my mouth and gasped. He looked dead. At the head of his bed sat a machine I couldn't remember seeing the last time. Then I realized it was a crash cart. A nurse pulled up a chair for me as tears streamed down my face. She explained he was heavily sedated so as not to move around, and made sure I understood the crash cart was merely a precaution.

Day after day I sat in the ICU. They kept him unconscious. I read to him, sang to him, and stroked his hands and forehead, willing him not to give up. I asked God to continue holding him safely in his arms. It was all I could do.

Instead of a week, Mathew stayed a month. He didn't bounce back as fast as they'd thought, but a month later I was more comfortable taking him home. Surprisingly, we fell right back into our old routine, and before long I was enjoying my little man again.

Yet another month went by. Our day started out as usual, up at the crack of dawn, morning meds to draw up, vital signs to chart, one injection to administer, and fill his feeding pump. While changing his diaper I noticed a spot of blood on his undershirt. Looking closer I was astonished to see what looked like wires protruding from his chest. We headed for the hospital.

By this time my local emergency room knew Mathew and I, but because of his issues, they didn't like to see us come through their doors. This day he presented with just as complex a problem, wires coming through his chest at the surgery site.

When I was learning to care for Mathew, I was always told to first look at the baby. Was he in apparent distress, an indication of urgency. He was not, but just the thought of wires sticking out was more than a bit distressing for me! After they made several conference calls to Children's Hospital, I was cleared to drive him there myself. Half way over, in heavy traffic, and with nowhere to pull over, should the need arise, I burst into tears thinking, what am I doing? This baby's life is so fragile. I'm *just a Mom*, how can I be doing this?

While I was coming apart at the seams, Mathew seemed to be enjoying the car ride, calm and quiet, not the least bit upset. When I realized he was fine, I was able to get a grip on myself. In hindsight I must have had a small panic attack. From that day forward I carried a bright red scarf in my car. If I needed immediate help I'd call 911, give the year, make, and color of my car and hang the identifiable scarf out the window to blow in the wind. That way police or ambulance drivers would be more likely to spot my car in heavy traffic.

When we got to the hospital, doctors were waiting. Mathew was examined and a mere twenty minutes later we were back on the road heading home, one hundred and forty miles round trip! His surgeon explained that the exposed wires worked as a twisty you often find on plastic bags. When open heart surgery is done, they must first break through the breast bone. Because further surgeries were inevitable, a wire twisty was used to close it, making the next procedure easier on Mathew. He was in no immediate danger. The twisty remained tight, but the wires were too long and piercing the skin. I was instructed to keep a sterile dressing over the site for the next week, at which time he had a scheduled heart catheterization. They would anesthetize him for that and take care of the exposed wires at the same time.

Mathew and I were inseparable. Taking care of him was a huge responsibility. Though fraught with feelings of inadequacy and fear, the rewards were great. However, I was reaching my breaking point and running on minimal sleep. Something had to change.

His birth mother relinquished her parental rights. She was homeless, young, and could not care for her son. Always in the back of my mind was, who will be there for Mathew, will he find a forever family?

Sadly, I observed time and again, people looking to adopt perfect children. Who would want Mathew? Who would want to take a child who needed a new heart? Who would want a child with a lifetime of *what ifs?* Who? It was one of many worrying thoughts that crossed my mind every day. I saw Mathew as the most perfect, awe-inspiring little boy. It was as if I was seeing him from the inside out and people looking to adopt would see him from the outside in. I saw his gentle nature, his sweetness, and his strength. The illness was secondary to who he was, but they would see the child who looked ill, blue, with massive scars covering his chest, and who tired easily. They would see his monitors, and at times, his oxygen equipment. They wouldn't be interested long enough to see who he was on the inside, *perfect*. The whole process of adoption for Mathew scared me. The alternative would have been a care facility, no doubt for the rest of his life. I wouldn't even entertain that possibility and put it out of my mind.

Weeks later I was surprised when his social worker called to say a family wanted to meet him. My first thought was, when they speak to his cardiologist they'll be out the door in a flash. It was too much to hope for. Instead, they came for a visit, and in their words, "fell in love." I remained skeptical. I desperately didn't want to be disappointed, so I wouldn't allow myself to think there could be a happy ending.

During the visit, neither Mom nor Dad seemed afraid of him, they weren't even nervous. I was struck by their gentleness, they were loving and kind. I realized I liked them, and best of all, she was a nurse. I knew in my heart it was meant to be, and sure enough, a week later I received word from the state. Mathew was going to have his very own *forever family,* complete with a dog and a couple of years later, a beautiful baby sister. They are wonderful and Mathew is thriving, though he's been through another open heart surgery to repair a leaking valve that worried his doctors since he lived with me. I visited him the day prior to the procedure at a park near Children's Hospital. I usually get over to see him once or twice a year and it's always a special time. This particular day he was playing with other children but not with as much gusto. In his first weeks of life doctors believe he had one or two strokes. As a result, his left side was weakened and his stride slightly impaired. I noticed it made climbing the stairs on the slide harder for him, and he struggled to run and keep up with the other children. His Mom told me his heart filled three quarters of his chest. Normally, it would be the size of his fist which isn't very big on a four year old.

The following day he was wheeled into the operating room where doctors removed four fifths of his heart and repaired the leaky valve. Just as we all ventured a sigh of relief, bleeding became a major problem. My tiny angel was returned to surgery where doctors rushed to stabilize him and bring the bleeding under control. The following day they discovered a blood clot which they were able to resolve with medications.

As bad as it was, and as bad as it could have gotten, within a few days Mathew was out of bed with a toy vacuum cleaner vacuuming the hall outside his room! He told one of the nurses he'd be happy to go to her house and vacuum as well! When I looked in on him asleep later that afternoon, I was taken aback by the sight of his chest. A scar from his throat to his navel, and as in times past, a formidable array of sophisticated machines, some turned on, others on stand by. So much for a little boy to endure.

A few days later I visited again, only this time he was out with his Mom cruising around the hospital in a Kid's Hospital *Taxi*. On his return I marveled at how much better he looked. His color was good, and he seemed to light up when he saw me. Of course it helped that he spotted my gift bag with Spiderman sticking out the top.

Many doctors, as well as family members, come together to determine what's best for Mathew. It's all about faith, love, and trust.

Within a few days he went home and his Mom called to tell me he was doing great. We are ever hopeful he will continue to fight his brave battle.

If love has anything to do with it, Mathew will be with us all for a very long time.

25

Claire

"Once you see it, you connect with it."
—**Naomi Watts, US AIDS Envoy**

Claire was with me a year and a half when her social worker told me to have her tested for HIV.

I remember back to the day I got the call "Mary, will you take this baby?" I grabbed the car seat and headed out the door.

Claire was a vision, petite, with a tiny wisp of blonde hair, blue eyes, and skin like porcelain. She was three weeks old, drug affected, and going through severe withdrawals.

A baby left my care just hours earlier. I barely had time to sterilize the bottles and wash the linens. It happened like that sometimes. I was thrilled to have a little girl for a change. I'd get to use the basket full of ribbons for her hair, and the pretty little smocked dresses in the closet. I couldn't wait to show her off to my friend.

When babies came into care, we were required to have them checked by a pediatrician within a day or two. I noticed something wasn't quite right with her left eye, and her pediatrician suggested a specialist take a look. Within the week I learned her eye was blind. Aside from the lingering effects of drugs in utero, fitful screaming nights, tremors, and poor eating initially, she began to do very well. By two months old she was strong enough to have exploratory surgery on her eye to determine if sight could be acquired. Sadly it could not, there was no optic nerve.

As the months went by any signs of failure to thrive were dissipating, and Claire was quite the little character. She had more fire in her than I'd seen in a baby for a long time. She gave me a run for my money, and it was wonderful to sit back and watch the little dynamo in action. For certain one eye wasn't going to slow her down. Everything was a challenge, and she was prepared to meet each one head on. She never went around anything, it was always up and over, or through! I had to be on my toes 24/7 but loved every minute of it. Her favorite pastime was blowing on her harmonica, so much so I took to hiding it from time to time just to remain sane.

When she turned ten months old, it was time for the next step in dealing with her blind eye. Left as it was, it would look different, shrunken, and other children would likely make fun of her.

Her oculist planned to outfit her with a scleral cap, a prosthetic device fitted over the blind eye and painted to match the sighted eye. I would have to put it in place every morning and remove it at bedtime. It sounded simple enough, but I soon found out it was no easy task with an active infant in my arms. The following day I had a major problem on my hands.

Within thirty minutes of putting the cap in, Claire was unconscious. Thinking I must have done something wrong I rushed her to the doctor. It was in properly. Two days and two tries later, it was apparent her semi-conscious state was related to wearing the scleral cap, her body's way of rejecting the prosthetic device. She wouldn't be able to wear it.

As all this was playing out, a family from out of state came forward, interested in meeting her with the intent to adopt. Initial paperwork was begun, and a visit planned. Claire was starting to learn to walk, at that adorable stage of first faltering steps. How would they not fall in love with her.

The day of their visit I was apprehensive. What if I didn't like them? As it turned out, my worries were needless. She had a lovely time playing, talking, and getting to know each other. It felt right.

While the adoption paperwork moved forward, we had more visits to make sure Claire and her prospective new parents were comfortable with each other. Included in the paperwork were specific instructions for her new family to look into further options for her eye. The state would stay involved until it was resolved. Claire turned eighteen months old, and just before her adoption was finalized, we received a call that had a profound effect on *all* our lives. The state had reason to believe Claire was HIV positive. We were told to have her tested.

My world dropped out from under me. All I could think about was Claire, my family, and two other foster babies I'd had for short periods of time while she was with me. I didn't know much about HIV other than what I'd heard on television and read in newspaper articles. Once I was able to comprehend the gravity of the situation, I arranged for the test.

It was like any other blood draw. If you have children you may recall the nurse almost always asking you to hold a piece of gauze over the draw site until the bleeding stopped. When she asked me to do the same, I looked up at her and said, "Do you really think that's wise? you're testing her for HIV; You're the one wearing gloves." She acquiesced.

There are no words to describe how I got through the next *three* days as I waited for the test result to come back. Today it would take only minutes. I thought about Claire cracking the television control guard in an attempt to push the buttons. She cut her finger twice trying. Each time I wiped away the few drops of blood thinking nothing of it. I thought about the doctors who operated on her eye, they could have been exposed as well. So many occurrences came to mind as the days dragged on, I also thought, how could this have happened? I vacillated between being scared, and being angry.

Time dragged on for what seemed like weeks, when finally, the call came, Claire *did not* have HIV. I cried, the sense of relief overwhelming me.

Life returned to what I can only describe as a guarded normal. Our joy and laughter following the scare was short lived, her adoption was only weeks away.

I was so happy for Claire when her big day came. She was going to have her own forever family. I can still see her running around in her plaid dress with matching hat, lacy white pantaloons, and black Mary-Jane shoes. It was her day.

As I kissed her goodbye, I held her close and whispered a promise in her ear. Today, ten years later I'm still trying to keep my promise.

My heart cried for Claire when she left. I longed to hear the harmonica. I felt no one could keep her safe as well as I could. When she called "Ma Ma," did she go looking for me? I questioned if I could continue as a foster mother. Added to that, my anger kept coming back. How could this *thing* called HIV have touched my world? I thought it only happened to others, continents away, not here in my small town, in my sweet innocent little baby. The more I thought about it, the more I wanted to know, the more I *had* to know. I set out to educate myself.

When a baby is born, the mother passes her antibodies to the child. They circulate within the baby for about six months, protecting its health until they have stored antibodies of its own, then the mother's dissipate. In much the same way, if the mother has HIV, it is passed to her baby. There is however, a window of opportunity when, if treated, the virus can be stopped before it settles in the baby to stay, starting during labor, and within twelve hours following delivery.

Claire's mother was known to have a drug problem, lived a reckless and dangerous lifestyle, and put her baby at great risk. The state also put her at risk knowing her circumstances and not having her tested at birth. I was horrified to learn they knew of the possibility soon after she was born but neglected to tell me until she was ready to be adopted. I felt allowing the cloak secrecy, under the guise of privacy, was in itself a form of child abuse. Had she tested positive, antiretroviral treatment could have saved her from contracting the HIV virus. She was now eighteen months old, long past the window of opportunity. The state later told a reporter *not* telling me she *might* have HIV was, in their words, *"an oversight."* In my mind it was incomprehensible. There was no room for glossing over, waltzing around, or shifting responsibility. Why wouldn't anyone step up to the plate for the safety of all concerned? Make no mistake, we were dealing with a life-threatening disease. I had to do something before another child, and another foster family were in my position. But where would I start? I was *just a Mom*. Well, I started in the *wrong* place.

I wrote a lengthy letter to my congressman who promptly responded. He was very interested in my issue, but pointed out it was a state matter, not federal, and suggested who I might get in touch with. After that I put my pen to paper countless times getting my message out, and asking for help. I wanted it made law that my babies be tested if they were born drug positive, and their mother's HIV status was unknown. I was a firm believer when taking these adorable, sweet infants into my home, and my life, I was there for the long haul; whatever it took to make their lives better; whatever it took to get them healthy; and whatever it took to keep them safe. They had no voice, I did. If I had to shout, I would do that too,

In early 2004 my first bill was introduced in the legislature that required testing. It passed as a revised bill that called for a study to determine if testing was necessary. A panel of experts from across the state convened. They studied several diseases that could be transferred from mother to child, and reported their findings back to the legislature. *The only one* they concluded should be tested for was HIV. Being *just a mom*, I thought, "I did it, I won." I didn't. It was a step forward, but I needed enabling legislation. I picked up my pen again, this time to the Bill and Melinda Gates Foundation. Having heard so much about their involvement with the HIV/AIDS epidemic in other parts of the world, I thought surely they would help me. Instead of a world away, I lived just down the road from them. I asked for a letter of support, or someone to testify in favor of my bill. Their reply: "*Although we appreciate the value of your request, it falls outside our current program guidelines. Unfortunately we will not be able to provide the requested testimony or a letter of support. We wish you the best in your endeavors.*" I was disheartened but not ready to give up. If anything, their reply strengthened my resolve to push forward.

I picked up my trusted pen again and wrote to the Clinton Foundation asking for a letter of support. I'd heard about the wondrous things they too were doing, and their involvement with HIV/AIDS issues. Within the week I received their reply.

"*On behalf of President Clinton, thank you for requesting his endorsement of mandatory HIV/AIDS testing of foster children. I regret that the former President is unable to provide such an endorsement. He would want to be closely involved in any project to which he lends his support or name, and his current set of obligations does no allow him to devote the necessary amount of time to this endeavor.*"

I was more than a little disappointed and becoming disillusioned. I went back to the only thing I could rely on, myself.

I spoke at luncheons and various meetings. I had to let the public know what my babies were up against, what their futures could have in store. I discovered complacency in my community. Many didn't seem to want to know, as if somehow it might put them at risk. I had my jeweler make a pin in bold half inch letters for my lapel that simply said HIV. I wore it everywhere hoping people would take notice and ask questions. Instead, most shied away from me.

Quite by accident one day, I read about the Elizabeth Glaser Pediatric AIDS Foundation. You guessed it, I got out my trusty pen, again, and asked for their support. I thought surely they were the answer to my prayers. It was not to be. *"Since receiving your letter the Foundation's Public Policy team has been receiving your situation. The issue of testing infants placed in foster care for HIV/AIDS falls outside the scope of the Foundation's work."* Why couldn't I get anyone to help?

I may have been *just a mom*, but I was learning. Over the next three years, three more bills were introduced on my behalf advocating for my babies. With a baby under one arm and my briefcase under the other, I testified in committee hearings for each one. There came a point when discussions became so contentious it created an uproar. Another time it was election year and no one wanted to take on such a controversial bill. Still another year money was the hold up. A fiscal note was attached and the government was pinching pennies. It didn't make it out of committee. Money still seems to be a problem. It's important to note here, testing itself is not expensive, under twenty dollars. What makes the cost rise is clerical support staff and the social workers' time. It is also important to note, there are still people in our community who fear mandatory testing of any kind regarding HIV. Add to that, current privacy issues. However, babies are the only segment of the population where HIV can be stopped. What this all comes down to is, with early testing, babies who are positive at birth, can be negative by eighteen months old. Intervention is key.

Foster parents were told to use universal precautions and treat all children as if they had it. I refused to do that. My babies needed touch, they needed to feel the warmth of my arms. I could not wear gloves simply because they *might* be HIV positive. I was peed on, puked on, and pooped on, on a regular basis. Slobbery wet kisses, and holding blood-soaked gauze over bleeding injection sights was par for the course and routine for me. Just trimming tiny finger nails could elicit a trail of blood, as could a skinned knee when any child was leaning to walk. If I were to handle my babies as if they all had HIV would have been a disservice to them. For me, the old adage, *"What you don't know won't hurt you* "became" *What you don't know may kill you."*

I went on to foster more babies, but with more informed conviction. I took nothing for granted. Thereafter, every time I picked up a new baby I asked myself, "Do I feel lucky today?" I continued to fight for them, but no longer felt I was *just a mom.*

A few months after Claire left, her mom called to give me an update on how they were doing. Claire was adjusting well to the move with no concerns other than her blind eye. They contacted a specialist who had experience with her problem. The plan was to do a complete evisceration, meaning the removal of the entire eye. In its place he would insert a metal pin and sew the eye closed for a month to heal. A new scleral cap would be fitted over the pin then painted to match the sighted eye. The amazing part was both eyes would move in sync, no one would ever guess one was blind. She wore protective glasses on the playground to ensure the safety of the sighted eye. Mom later reported Claire never experienced any problems with her new high tech eye, though she did say the family dog protested greatly when she tried to insert the old cap in its eye on more than one occasion!

The day before Thanksgiving, two years later, I received a call from the placement desk. Claire had a new baby sister and the state wanted to know if I would be her foster mother. Early the next day I welcomed baby Sabrina into my life.

We had an instant bond and she was every inch a carbon copy of Claire. It was a special Thanksgiving for me, my blessings were many. Another baby was safely taken off the streets. Sabrina presented with the same HIV risk as did Claire, so I asked for testing. Sadly nothing had changed, I couldn't have it done.

My time with Sabrina was wonderful though she didn't stay long. The family who adopted Claire wanted to adopt her as well. I was overjoyed. Visits were scheduled, paperwork completed, and by four months old, Sabrina left with her *forever family*. Those were always bitter sweet days for me.

Barely a year later, I received another call, Claire and Sabrina had a new baby brother, Jackson. Would I take him? Though it broke my heart to say no, I was licensed to have two babies at a time and both my nurseries were in use. Baby Jackson went to another foster home, and in the ensuing months the family who adopted his sisters adopted him as well. It was a happy ending, they'd be together forever. As for me, Claire, Sabrina, and Jackson will always be just a heartbeat away.

Tucker

Sometimes what you see is harder to grasp than what you hear. This day, the state called to tell me about a little guy, Tucker, a couple of months old in a military hospital. Could I take him into my care? For the first time in a long time, this baby was not going through withdrawals. Instead, Tucker had two broken legs, evidence of healed fractures in both arms, and a concussion. I headed to the hospital. To see this tiny infant in a brace from his neck to his toes broke my heart. One look into his eyes and I knew I could care for him no matter what the doctor said. He needed to be loved, held, and nurtured. I could do that and he would heal on the inside as well as on the outside.

Staff gave me all the information and instructions I needed for dealing with so many broken bones and not causing further discomfort when I put his brace on, changed his diaper, or bathed him. Two days later I took him home. We were already buddies. Before long wherever I went, he went, including my weekly meeting in the legislature. It wasn't uncommon for me to show up with a baby from time to time. The bills we discussed pertained to children within the foster care system.

This one particular day a gentleman at the meeting asked if he could hold the baby. I hesitated at first, then agreed, but cautioned him to use special care around his legs. No one could see his brace under his clothing. He asked why so I told him, "Both legs are broken."

The man started to cry. The room echoed deafening silence as tears streamed down the sides of his face. He gently placed Tucker back in my arms then turned and left the room overcome with emotion. You could have heard a pin drop. One of the bills up for discussion that day spoke to funding for children of abuse. By sheer coincidence Tucker was there with me. It was a powerful moment, one I will never forget, and I daresay others in attendance won't either.

Tucker was a joy in my life. It took a while before I could see past the intimidating brace and his reason for wearing it.

This case was particularly difficult for me because it was implied the father was responsible for Tucker's injuries. When I finally got to meet him he was in uniform. I remember feeling every fiber of my being screaming out at him. How could he wear the uniform of his country, the same uniform I once wore, and inflict such egregious injuries on his infant son. I couldn't come to terms with it, but I knew in order to help Tucker, and be there for him, I'd have to change my focus. As a foster parent the very nature of the job can be shocking as is most often the case. I had to accept it, and put it in a special place deep within me. I had to put Tucker first, and he didn't need to see me weepy and sad all the time. I learned to see beyond *my* hurt and find *his* joy. I found the child.

Soon he was playing, and interacting. He was healing and so was I. I never knew the outcome of Tucker's case other than relatives came forward and shortly thereafter he left my care. He would be safe and continue to heal. I was thankful he was with extended members of his family, and didn't stay in the system for a long period of time. He is often in my thoughts and forever in my heart.

Grayson

They say all babies are beautiful. That's not true. My babies were breath-taking. That's how I met Grayson, he took my breath away.

As I entered the pediatric wing of Children's Hospital I was apprehensive. I'd been given limited information about this little guy, and was asked if I'd take him. It seemed the babies I was taking now were sicker and sicker, but I always had the opportunity to meet with doctors before deciding if I felt confident enough to go forward with placement.

He was an identical twin, born prematurely, and both weighed barely two pounds. Baby Noah was small, but in good health. Grayson however, was in critical condition. He had severe gastrointestinal issues, and was on life support for a period of time. A portion of his intestines were placed outside his abdomen, and a very large scar covered the lower half of his stomach. There was no question *if* I could care for him, he'd already walked right into my heart and made himself comfortable.

In the ensuing weeks I made, at times, daily trips to the hospital in Seattle, some seventy miles away, not only to get to know him, but to observe and learn how to care for him. He had to be closely monitored, required many medications, and needed lots of attention and nurturing. I knew little of his circumstances other than his birth parents didn't feel able to care for two infants, in particular one with serious medical issues.

Grayson remained in the hospital for four months. Noah stayed two, then released to the care of his parents once he reached a healthy four pounds.

In the winter of that year Grayson and I began what became a life-changing journey for both of us.

It always amazed me over the years that no matter what the circumstances, no matter how ill, or how severe their injuries were, my babies always seemed comfortable and trusting coming into my world. It made my job that much more rewarding. It was, and still is my belief, that everyone knows if they are loved, the driving force my babies had to feel to get healthy and strong.

The plan was for me to have Grayson until the state decided their next course of action now that both babies were out of the hospital. Weekly visitations were scheduled so the twins could feel their special bond, but it soon became apparent it wasn't a priority. Visits were few and far between, and family members could not even be reached when Grayson was rushed into emergency surgery. Hospital staff voiced their concerns to the Department of Social and Health Services.

Grayson and I made regular trips back to the hospital for various procedures and checkups. Occasionally his father showed up with Noah and we talked about how the twins were doing, though I never met their mother.

At home Grayson was making great progress. I made him the center of my universe. With my own children now out on their own, I had all the time in the world to lavish on him. Having spent so many days in the hospital, he was still on their hours and routines, one in particular. Every night, regular as clockwork, he knew when it was change of shift time and the nurses made their rounds. That meant checking medications, monitors, and taking vitals, along with a bit of chit chat. When I brought him home he figured I should be up for it as well… at 4:00 am! I'd change his diaper, talk to him, feed him, then he'd roll over and go right back to sleep. He did that every night until the day he left. He is now five years old and I would venture to guess at 4:00 am he still wakes and wants a chat and a snack.

It didn't take long for Grayson and I to become buddies. When there was a little one to care for I was the happiest. I felt fortunate and blessed to be part of his life. I was, however, becoming increasingly concerned when we met with his dad and brother. Noah looked gaunt and pale. He was very thin and didn't seem to react appropriately to his surroundings. His eyes were either in a fixed stare, or rolling as if he couldn't focus. He was beginning to look sicker than Grayson. I was a mandated reporter and as such, if I saw or heard something that might endanger a child, I was required by law to report it to Child Protective Services. I set up a meeting to voice my concerns and strongly indicated that I felt something was wrong. I told them I didn't think Noah was in a *good place*. They took it under advisement and thanked me for bringing it to their attention. On two or three occasions over the following weeks I reiterated my concerns to a CPS worker.

Days later, following a checkup with Grayson and his doctors, I went by the Department of Social and Health Services office to tell his social worker how he was getting along. I thought it was odd that his father hadn't showed up that day for our appointment. Instead of his social worker, a CPS worker came over and asked to speak to me in an adjacent room. In what seemed a moment in time, the world was forever changed for Grayson and I. Baby Noah, the healthy twin, had been beaten to death by his mother.

I felt the blood drain from my head. I went numb as tears streamed down my face. Clutching Grayson tight in my arms, I started to leave the room then turned and in between uncontrollable sobs I shouted "Why didn't you listen to me?" She didn't say a word.

After a long drive home, and many tears, I sat with Grayson and turned on the news. Noah's murder was the lead story.

He'd been crying and wouldn't lie still to have his diaper changed. His mother inflicted blunt force trauma to his head, and two days later, with

39

no medical intervention, he died. He bled to death internally. He was only five months old. On that day a part of me died as well, but another part of me was born.

My anger erupted in a fury. I contacted the Office of the Ombudsman. They operate in conjunction with the Governor's Office to obtain independent and impartial review of decisions made by the Department of Social and Health Services, as well as other state child welfare agencies. I was prepared to blow everything right out of the water. I made it known I would sue the state on behalf of Grayson for wrongful death. I would go to the media. The public needed to know how and why this innocent life was taken.

It was hard to look at Grayson in the days following without crying. He and Noah had struggled so hard to come into the world, only to be separated forever.

I consulted with seven attorneys. A wrongful death suit was out of the question, but I could proceed with a survivor – ship suit. I'd have to prepare myself for what they called, "A high profile case with a great deal of media coverage."

I weighed the possible outcomes, what I wanted, and my best chance of getting satisfaction. It was all for Grayson; through him, a greater awareness of the needs of every child in the system. Policies within Child Protective Services needed to change.

I tried speaking with legislators. Being *just a mom*, I hadn't realized the threat of litigation meant they wouldn't talk with me. In the end I chose to work within the system to change the system. The ramifications would be more for reaching and benefit all children in foster care.

In the Ombudsman's report to the legislature, 158 children died that reporting period, whose families had an open case with DSHS at the time of death or within a year prior to death. Everyone has the power to effect policy changes and we are responsible for *all* children. Certainly mother struck the fatal blow; but had Child Protective Services intervened as expected, she would never have had the opportunity.

Today, five years later, as I put my pencil to paper and relive that day, it's as if it were yesterday. The tears, the numb feeling, the pain, all come to the forefront and my body aches. I'd held Noah in my arms, looked into his eyes and felt his heartbeat. Until the day I die I will always feel I could have done more.

When children are unable to be placed with their parents, for whatever reason, the first place the state looks for a caregiver is other family members. This is done with thorough safety checks, background investigations, and home studies. It's time consuming and justifiably so. In Grayson's case, a relative agreed to take him believing the father would eventually step up to the plate. For this reason I was concerned about his placement with her and insisted they be documented and kept on file. I was overly protective because I loved him so much.

At the same time the relative search was going on, Noah's death was under investigation. That included a fatality review board. I made it my business to address its members with Grayson in my arms. I'd learned over the years that putting a face to an issue had more impact than volumes of numbers, facts, and suppositions. I introduced myself and Grayson, and told them to look closely at him because, when they were looking at Grayson, they were looking at Noah, his identical twin. The board then deliberated, concluded their findings and made it known why Noah died.

The report revealed his home had many services in place provided by the State and designed to aid the family in preparation for both babies' return. The service providers working in the home had concerns, but failed to

41

communicate them to authorities. As a result, Noah died from a lack of communication.

In due course, the birth mom went to trial and was sentenced to twenty three years and four months in federal prison. With good conduct she'd likely serve a third of that. It was, and still is my belief, a few others should be sharing her cell.

I can still see Grayson playing on the floor and learning to crawl. How frustrated he'd get when his initial tries put him in reverse or in circles. It was so funny, at the same time so cute. I videoed his attempts everyday till one day he got it, and I got it all on video. He was moving forward.

The relative flew into town and shadowed Grayson and I, noting everything about his care. When she was comfortable with him, and he with her in his life, they were given the go ahead and Grayson left. He was a few days shy of one year old. A year later I received a call telling me she'd adopted him and he was doing well.

Every year on the anniversary of Noah's death, I place a bouquet of Baby's Breath on the altar in my chapel, with a note asking he be remembered in prayer.

I followed through, I had to know how the system would change following Noah's cruel and senseless death. What I got was a lengthy list of requirements and meetings that social workers had to adhere to while assisting the department in making appropriate decisions. The goal being to develop the best plan for the child's safety and permanency. In many cases the use of shared planning opportunities is now required by policy, and always encouraged by supervisors and management. In Noah's case, individual employee's actions were reviewed and resulted in counseling and re-training. Some workers were required to attend a summer safety program involving working with vulnerable children. Statewide training modules were adopted, and a new curriculum was developed.

No one ever told me *why* the system failed baby Noah.

Joey

I was washing dishes one morning when I received the call. Could I take this baby? Joey, five days old and still in the hospital needed placement. Both his birth parents had mental health issues and staff raised concerns about their ability to safely care for a newborn. The state intervened until more was known and contacted me.

My home was always ready to take a child. I was thrilled, so much so that later in the day, when I left to pick him up I took a diaper with me, but forgot his clothes!

I never knew how long babies would be with me but, as it turned out, this young man stayed the longest of any of them, five years.

My days were full keeping house and caring for a newborn. Joey wasn't what you'd call *an easy baby* at first. He was hard to entertain, and didn't take an interest in things around him. Unless I was engaging with him, he cried most of the time. I tried surrounding him with enough toys to stock a toy store, but it was as if he didn't see them. He rarely picked up a toy, and when he did, he only touched it with his index fingers. As the days went by I was getting increasingly concerned. Joey wasn't meeting the usual infant milestones.

I remembered hearing about a local birth-to-three program for children with special needs, and decided it was time to get their input. A few days later, two of their staff members were at my home to meet and observe Joey. About the same time I had a follow-up with his pediatrician who recommended

I set up an appointment with a developmental specialist at Children's Hospital. Extensive testing began, and I was called in for the evaluation results.

I will never forget the crushing feeling that engulfed me when his doctor told me he was developmentally disabled. Not quite sure what that meant, I asked how we could *fix it.* "He's profoundly retarded she said, it cannot be fixed."

Tears flooded my eyes, and in between sobs I said, "But he can't be, he's so sweet." My heart and brain couldn't wrap around the devastating news.

I took Joey home and loved him even more. As reality set in I did everything possible to help him progress. Special classes were set up in the birth-to-three program, and therapists came into my home to work with him on cognitive skills, speech, and physical therapy. Joey was more content, fussed less, but still could do little for himself. I was told he might never walk, speak, or feed himself, as well as the possibility he may always be diapered. Amid all this doom and gloom his constant crying all but stopped, replaced with an ever-present smile that lit up the world. Everyone in town came to know Joey, and heaven forbid I be seen out without him in tow. He belonged to the community, they embraced him, they adored him.

I started taking sign language classes hoping to teach him a way to communicate. I signed almost everything never knowing how much he understood. Soon he made it clear he liked me to *talk* with my hands. He'd grab them and push them to my chest. Over time he signed two words back, *more* and *sing. More* took encouragement and he'd comply, but *sing* he fully understood and signed it every time I sat down. If I wanted his attention all I had to do was ask in a singing sort of way. He would respond and I was amazed. It became my way of connecting with him.

Things I'd always taken for granted in other children, I was now trying to find ways to teach him, like eating solid foods. It took months. With our first try he wouldn't even move his lips. Every day I prepared his meals in the same way, three times a day, until at eight months old he took the food in and swallowed. When it came time for stage two foods, which have a chunkier consistency, he wouldn't swallow. He liked everything I prepared for the family as long as it went in the blender first. When he started cutting teeth I offered him big hard baby cookies that resembled a cigar. They were designed to aid the painful process and sooth the gums. It took repeated tries every day for weeks just to get one in his mouth. To do that, I gently rubbed it up his arm every day, getting closer and closer, until he accepted it and bit down. That was how I learned to help Joey, trial and error. I had to approach things in a different way.

His first teacher in the birth-to-three program felt he'd never learn to walk. If I had anything to do with it he would. It became the focus of every day, followed by abundant praise. It took a long time, hard work, and again persistence, but at age two and a half Joey walked up to his teacher and smiled. The look on both their faces was priceless. It was well worth the wait.

Transitions were always stumbling blocks. Out of the car, into a buggy, then into a store being one of the hardest for my little man. I enlisted the aid of a big red wagon. It helped that I drove a van so there was plenty of space. I'd leave him in his car seat then place the car seat in the wagon. It went smoothly and once he was comfortable with that approach I was able to get him from the car seat straight into the buggy. I think he just knew I wasn't going to relent because shopping was inevitable in my world. Bless his heart, I bugged him everywhere and he soon learned to love being out and about. I was so proud of him.

When he outgrew the biggest buggy on the market, Children's Hospital outfitted him with a special one because he still often collapsed and couldn't get up. He was getting too big for me to carry as well. His new one looked a bit like a wheel chair, but it had a certain pizzazz. It also had a hefty price tag, $2,000! Fortunately, the state picked up the tab.

Before I knew it, Joey outgrew his crib. I wanted the transition to a big bed to be smooth, so I gave it a great deal of thought, then hired a handy man to reconfigure the crib to meet his needs. He removed one side and placed the mattress on the floor. This way Joey could get in and out by himself, still feel safe, and not get hurt. All my good intentions backfired. He cried and cried and wouldn't sleep. Clearly he didn't like my plan. Two nights later I brought in a regular twin size bed with a safety rail along one side and placed the other side along the wall. Problem solved. He took to it right away and it was never an issue again. He showed me who the clever one really was.

When I went anywhere with Joey, I could always rely on him to get us back to our car, in any parking lot, whether or not we'd ever been there before. I'd just say "Find Joey's car," and he'd lead me right to it with no hesitation. I often wondered just how disabled he really was.

His therapist thought it time to teach him cause and effect. Because he wouldn't play with toys, entertaining him continued to be a big issue. He did however love Sesame Street and similar programs on television. Her plan was to use the television to teach this concept. A big red button, about the size of a saucer, was connected to the T.V. and a timer turned it off every so many minutes. Joey was to learn that if he pushed the button, his show would automatically come right back on. The therapist explained to me it could take several days or more for him to learn, and perhaps he might never grasp the concept. We would try. Within fifteen minutes Joey knew how to get Big Bird back on the screen, as well as how to push a video in and start his own show! I was continually amazed at what he could do, now, versus what he couldn't do not long before.

As Joey got older, and it was determined he couldn't be raised by his birth parents, a search for a family began. Though I loved him dearly, I didn't feel up to the task. I was getting up there in years, and his care was immense and lifelong. Letting him go was in his best interest.

As luck would have it, a young woman clear across the country saw his picture and a brief history about him online. In her words, that day she fell in love and wanted to meet him.

After many months, home studies, and tedious, time consuming background checks, Joey was on his first plane ride, going home with his new forever Mom. He was five years old. Two years ago, at age thirteen, they came back for a visit. What a wonderful time we had, though all too soon he had to leave *again*.

Today he is fifteen and such a handsome young man. He will always have limitations, but his smile, sweet nature, and gentle soul know no boundaries. He will always touch the hearts of those around him. He is a gift.

Ruby

When I remember back to baby Ruby I think, so tiny, so fragile, and so ill. Born premature to a drug addicted mother, she weighed 1.9 lbs, or 861 grams, going through withdrawals, and fighting to survive. Once she stabilized, the state asked if I would take her.

Her first weeks were spent in an incubator in the NICU where we first met. Babies born under these, and similar circumstances, are pretty much on their own. That is to say, hospital staff are all they know. Moms, Dads, and family members are not visiting on a daily basis, if at all. These babies, only hours old, are already finding their own strength, and going through pure hell. Were it not for the love and care from nurses and volunteers, they'd not even feel a warm and loving touch.

Ruby was fighting an even greater battle. She had chronic lung disease, was on oxygen, had a shunt placed in her brain, and had corrective heart surgery. Added to this newborn's monumental challenges, she often stopped breathing and was placed on a heart-lung monitor. To put this all into perspective, her battle was bigger than any you or I would likely fight in our lifetime.

When she reached four pounds, and was considered in stable condition, I brought her home. She was still so small I couldn't hold her in the crook of my arm for fear she'd fall through. It wasn't unusual for her monitor to alarm, day or night, so her doctors classified her as a *line of sight* baby, and I was relegated to sleeping a few feet away from her in the nursery. A car ride anywhere often meant pulling off to the side of the road to assist her when alarms went off, and making sure she'd started breathing again.

Ruby was a good baby and nothing short of gorgeous. I often joked I'd only take good looking, smart babies, who slept through the night, so she fit right in. I also painted out to her I was old so she should go easy on me. After the initial getting to know each other period, we ventured down to the mall to meet my friend Judy, also a foster mother. When I lifted Ruby out of the pram Judy gasped, shocked at how small and frail she looked.

Ruby stayed with me almost seven months. On one occasion I had to call the paramedics. I'd heard a strange noise, then realized she was choking, frothing around her mouth and nose, gasping for air. They transferred her to Children's Hospital where they determined she had been aspirating into her lungs. After a few days in the hospital, I brought her home with a thickening agent to add to her formula to prevent further recurrences. It was a scary time, but for me the shakes always came after the scare, when I had time to think about what *could* have happened. The family who had already adopted Ruby's twin siblings came forward wanting to adopt her as well. They'd have each other forever. It doesn't get any better than that.

While the time consuming paperwork went through, her new Mom made regular visits to bond with her. It was during the winter months, and that particular year we had an abundance of snow on the ground. It didn't stop her from traveling nearly four hours round trip, to snuggle and form a bond.

All too soon it was time for Ruby to leave, she was strong and healthy. My job was done. Now it was time to begin her new life, with her very own forever family as so many had done before her. She lives near enough that we see each other from time to time. She calls me, "Mama Mary." I'm honored by that.

José

José had a hole in his heart.

José weighed two pounds. His Mom was thirteen years old and he had a hole in his heart.

I entered Children's Hospital. It wasn't the first time I'd met machines before I met the baby. In the center of the room, nestled beneath a cozy blanket, and surrounded by blinking machines, lay baby José, eyes wide open just looking around as if he was expecting me. I turned back his covers. If this was what he looked like at four pounds, I couldn't imagine what he looked like at birth. His frail little body hadn't finished growing inside his mother's womb. His lungs were underdeveloped, and downy soft black hair called lanugo, still covered most of his face, back, and arms. He was two months old. I learned to brace myself over the years of fostering fragile newborns. Hospital staff didn't approach me as the mom who needed to be briefed in a kind and gentle manner about their child's condition. To them I was just the *foster mom*. Their sheer bluntness sometimes shocked and amazed me.

It's not uncommon for babies to be born with a hole in their heart. He would be monitored closely by a cardiologist with regular checkups, and the hole would likely close on its own with no problems or interventions. His respiratory issues had resolved in the ICU, and I was assured his *furry appearance* would as well. He was stable enough to be released to my care. Two days later I welcomed him into my world. I bought out my sizable collection of preemie attire, but even they were too big. I resorted to soft flannel nighties until he'd put on weight. His bibs didn't just cover his chest, they covered his entire body. He looked like a *spot* in the center of his crib.

Within a week I could tell he was going to be a happy, easy to care for little charmer with a gigantic smile that brightened the world. There was no doubt in my mind, he was a miracle, an angel walking in my life. As with all my babies, wherever I went, he went. I became quite adept at getting baby, buggy, and diaper bag out of the car in no time, then running between Washington's famous rain drops to get my errands done or just walking around the mall for a change of scenery.

Scheduled, supervised visits were set up with his mom and dad every week. Though very young, they were exceptionally attentive to José's every need. From South America, they spoke very little English, so an interpreter was present at each visit. I could see from the start this family was different. The way they held José, the way they spoke to him, and to each other, was unlike what I usually observed. They did everything for him with an abundance of love, expertise, and confidence. I finally had to ask how they learned to be such loving and caring parents.

Through her interpreter, Mom explained that in her country they didn't have services available for families as in America. Instead, whole families raised families. They learned from each other, from birth, generation to generation. I was impressed.

Visits were never missed by both parents, and José continued to thrive. It was refreshing to watch a hands-on-dad, even when it came to changing a messy diaper. Though José had a slower start in life, it didn't take him long to catch up, and he was soon right on track.

After nearly seven months in my care, his heart was healing, and he was healthy. The state's plan was to return him to his parents, if all went well, when mom turned fourteen. Of all the Moms I'd dealt with over the years, this Mom, having turned fourteen, was one of the best, if not *the* best. I know that sounds too young to take on the full time job of parenting, but I had no reservations.

The day came when I had to let him go. I held him close and looked into his eyes. I thanked him for being in my life, told him how much I loved him, then kissed him goodbye.

I learned from having José, what family really means, more importantly, how strong the weak really are.

53

Jane Doe

Our Christmas Baby

As the holiday season draws nearer, I remember back about eight years ago, to the day before Christmas. It was cold and wet, a small amount of snow still hugged the ground, as if desperate to hang on till Christmas day. A baby girl had only just left my care a few days before, so I purchased tickets to see The Nutcracker ballet in Seattle.

The morning of the performance, as I busied myself getting ready for a fun day in the city, I received a desperate call from the placement desk. A newborn baby girl needed a home until family matters could be resolved. Would I take her, and could I pick her up that afternoon?

I was thrilled at the thought of having a baby under my tree Christmas morning, provided I could pick her up that evening following the ballet. They agreed.

It was all I could do to concentrate on the dancers, I was that excited about her arrival. The only thing lacking were the labor pains and I was thankful for that. When the lights finally dimmed and the curtain came down, I dashed over to Nordstrom's to pick up a few gifts for her, then headed to the hospital with car seat in hand. What a special Christmas it was going to be. I couldn't wait to meet her. Instead, I was met by the head nurse who told me *she was gone.* Her birth mother hadn't done anything wrong, she was homeless and refused help. The hospital had no choice but to let her go, to the back seat of a car, on a frosty Christmas eve because, "Being homeless didn't make her a bad mother."

I never knew the baby's name, but I've never forgotten her. Every Christmas I place the same pair of white porcelain baby shoes on my tree just for her. They are the only ones, amid fifty pairs or more, from previous babies over the years, without a name. She is not forgotten.

Andrew

In December of 2001, I had another Christmas baby, Andrew.

A neighbor of his heard her dog's frantic barking which was unusual. They had a large piece of property, and the dog kept running back and forth along the fence in a frenzy. She grabbed her coat and went to see what was upsetting him so. As she got nearer she heard a baby's cries and there, dressed only in a thin sleeper, lying up against the fence, was a tiny baby. She picked it up and ran for help.

Andrew was airlifted to Children's Hospital where it was determined he had a broken leg and head injuries. The following day I brought him home. An investigation was underway, and I was asked to keep a low profile.

As events unfolded, the Mom next door had been resting while her baby and four year old autistic son were asleep. Unbeknownst to her, the older brother awoke and decided he didn't want the newest center of attention in the family. He later showed an investigator how he'd taken Andrew by the leg, bounced him down several stairs, out the front door, across the yard, and threw him over the fence. He then slipped back into the house and went to sleep. Mom knew nothing until the police came knocking.

Therapy sessions were set up for the young perpetrator, the family reunited within days, and precautions were put in place to avoid a recurrence. Andrew wasn't with me long, but as I recall, I kept bundling him up thinking he must still be cold.

Diego, Emily, and Gabriela

He was the sunshine in every day, the brightest star in all the night sky. Every baby who came into my life was special, but Diego was different. He was a gift. In March 2005 the call came, would I take this baby? Diego had made his entrance into the world, underweight, and suffering from the effects of his mother's heroin addiction. After forty eight hours of observation, doctors determined his withdrawals could be managed in a home environment with minimal intervention. Since most of my babies over the years were exposed to drugs, I had acquired a fair amount of hands on experience. There was no question if I would take *this* baby.

Everything was ready for the new arrival. Even the balloons I hung on the lamp post seemed to dance with excitement. Within hours I was meeting the new man in my life as Diego was placed in my arms.

Funny how Moms can be. He was wrinkled, scowling, his thick black hair stuck straight up, and he had a scream that reverberated throughout the entire wing of the hospital. I was smitten!

At just under four pounds, his skin lay on him in creases, the result of nutrition deprivation in utero. His birth mother used drugs more often than eating nourishing meals, but aside from that, compared to recent babies in my care, this little guy was healthy and I couldn't wait to bring him home.

First feedings were always a special time for me. The eye to eye contact, the quiet meeting of hearts, and a forever bond formed and tightly sealed. Diego filled his tummy in record time then snuggled close against my neck as I rocked him to sleep. All was right in the world.

He settled in nicely, and it wasn't long before we had a comfortable routine. As long as his diaper was dry, and his tummy full, he never complained, though I noticed he was quieter than most. It would take time to see the *real* Diego, as if his brain needed time to retool from the effects of the heroin.

By two months old I started seeing slight changes in his expressions and alertness, he was sleeping less, and following my every movement around the room. As I reached to pick him up one afternoon there it was, a smile! That was the day Diego became a different child. With the drugs out of his system, he went from passive and lethargic, to full speed ahead. At three months old he could carry on a baby talk conversation with me unlike any I'd had before. I can be long winded at times, but Diego could out talk me, bantering back and forth, seeming to understand everything I said, and giving me his opinion in return.

From no interaction at all, now he'd find ways to get my attention. Most often he'd squeal and use what I called his mechanical eyes. I could feel them watching me. All I had to do was glance in his direction and he'd erupt in giggles.

Our lives were soon going to change when the all too familiar call came, "Mary, will you take this baby too?" A little girl, two months old, recovering from pertussis (whooping cough), was ready to be released from the hospital. When I was assured Diego would not be in any danger of catching it, I agreed to take her, not knowing I would be sorely tested in the days ahead. That evening, Emily was delivered to my front door. What a sweetheart, blonde, blue-eyed, and cute as could be. Well on the road to recovery, I'd only have to give her one medication, the rest of her care would be consistent with any child her age. I wondered what Diego would think of her and having to share my attention. He was already tucked in for the night when she arrived, but the next morning he grew wide eyed when he heard another tiny squeal demanding breakfast. He looked at me as if to say, "Where did she come from, and is she staying?"

Once both tummies were full, I lay them on the carpet at opposite ends of the toy room. They kept stretching to see each other, so I moved them closer and closer until they were side by side and totally mesmerized with one another. My days were very busy. It was like having twins in the house. I had to remind myself from time-to-time to eat, and if they were napping, I'd close *one* eye. My life revolved around them. If I wasn't feeding, diapering, bathing, or playing with them, there was laundry, dishes, ironing, dusting, and if time allowed, taking a shower and combing my hair. A change of scenery kept everything in perspective, so at least twice a week I packed up the pair of them, the diaper bags, the bottles of formula, loaded up the car, and headed to the mall.

Many times over the years, I commented that my babies had halos over their heads because passersby were drawn to them. With these two it was no different. We seldom went more than a few feet before someone would stop and ask in which store I bought them! My snow white hair was a dead giveaway they weren't mine.

Over time I met people who wanted to believe they were my grandchildren rather than foster children. There were those who perceived them differently, as bedraggled, needy, and problematic kids. The majority though, fell in love, their hearts were touched, and it was always my hope one of them would consider becoming a foster parent.

Emily was still coughing quite a bit, but her doctor told me to expect that. On this day we had been at the mall for several hours, stopped at all my favorite stores, chatted with the employees and assured everyone the babies were doing well. Even the security guards checked on their progress and encouraged first smiles from each one. We had lunch, *people-watched* for a while, then headed home with a couple of cookies for *me* to enjoy later.

On this particular evening we were playing on the floor, Emily in her little recliner chair, and Diego on my lap, when I heard a strange noise. Emily appeared lifeless and blue. I could tell she wasn't breathing. Quickly laying Diego on the floor beside me, I grabbed Emily from her little chair and turned her over to begin CPR. As I did, the sudden fast movement triggered a loud gasp and she started screaming, her skin almost instantly pink again.

With the car keys in my mouth, and a baby under each arm, I headed for the car, the hospital was nearby.

Pertussis can be threatening in very young babies. Though her doctors thought she was out of the woods when she was released to my care, she wasn't. From the emergency room she was transferred to Children's Hospital to recuperate fully.

I will be forever thankful I was sitting beside her when she needed me most. It took a while to come to terms with the events of that day. Had she not started breathing when I turned her over could I have breathed life into her? Could I have saved her? Being trained doesn't always mean you can respond when put to the test. I questioned if I could continue as a foster mother. It was the most terrifying day of my life. I never heard anything more, other than relatives from out of state came forward to take care of her. It took almost losing her before family closed ranks to help her.

Diego still needed me. He was my focus now, my way of coping with the scare. He was getting more active, rolling his way around the house, laughing, chattering, and attempting to crawl. I'd sit for hours and just enjoy being with him. I missed him even when he was sleeping. I never knew one tiny child could be so captivating.

Though I had enough toys in the house to stock a toy store, Diego took a liking to matchbox cars, perhaps the better word would be *obsession*. I never saw him without one in each hand, even as he learned to crawl, and that wasn't easy!

I heard *vroom, vroom,* all day, it became his mantra. I set up his own little *garage* behind a chair in the family room. The window sill was line with trucks and cars. I couldn't always see him, but I sure could hear him. If I called his name he'd come flying around the corner of the chair on all fours, cars in hand, yelling, "Ma Ma, Ma Ma." I'd never seen such tiny arms and legs move as fast as his.

I was running three of four miles every day and Diego loved the time we spent together outdoors. Before long he'd be lunging in the jogging stroller trying to make it go faster, squealing with delight and giggling so hard he'd choke.

He often tried to imitate me when I winked at him, so I set out to teach him how to make *flirty eyes!* It was the most precious thing to watch him, both eyes blinking as fast as he could, and grinning from ear to ear.

It wasn't long before he was learning to walk. With cars in hand, he delighted in standing in front of the sofa as I coaxed him to move forward one or two steps. He always had an impish look about him, and while his initial tries were disasters and wipe-outs, it wasn't long before he was an expert in *walking and running 101*. Both gave him freedom, not to mention foster getaways when I was trying to catch him.

I observed with many of my drug affected infants, they were slower meeting the usual milestones within the first year. That wasn't the case with Diego, he was even a bit precocious, full speed ahead even.

Having mastered walking and running, he took up climbing. He reminded me of goats on the side of mountains in far off countries. If it was climbable, Diego climbed it. Up the wood stove, the fireplace, the furniture, and the television. He'd even pull out the drawers on the bottom of the stove to scale the front of it. Diego was a *can do* sort of guy. I couldn't let him out of my sight for a second. He had scheduled supervised visits with his father since birth, but never with his mother. He'd just turned one when they made the difficult decision to release him for adoption. Mom, who was pregnant again, wanted to say goodbye to her son.

The day of the visit Diego wouldn't leave my side, holding on tight. He didn't know who she was, and wouldn't go to her. Sadly, she understood, and told me she just wanted to see him once more before all the papers were signed. Her incredible pain was evident on her face. It was all I could do to hold back my own tears.

My days with Diego took on a different feel. I knew it wouldn't be long before someone would want to adopt him, and as I expected, only weeks later a family came forward.

How could I let him go? He was entrenched in my heart. Why couldn't he stay with me through high school, even college. I wanted to teach him to drive the cars he loved so much.

A visit was arranged with the family and the social worker. As it turned out, they voiced concerns about the shape of Diego's head, it was somewhat flat in the back because he consistently slept in the same position. I would go in his room several times before I went to bed each night, turn him over, but within minutes he'd move right back. The family who'd been interested in adopting him, thought it meant brain damage and couldn't be convinced otherwise. I'd seen this happen before, families wanting to adopt the *perfect* hand-picked child. How sad it made me feel. *Diego was perfect.* It was them who were too blind to see it.

At his next appointment with the pediatrician, I addressed the shape of his head. She wasn't concerned, but suggested a visit to Children's Hospital to have him evaluated. Doctors there felt he met the criteria for a medical helmet that would correct the shape within six months.

Some babies change their sleeping habits on their own and the shape corrects itself. That wasn't happening with Diego, so within the next month he was fitted with a helmet that made him look like a football player. He had to wear it twenty-four hours a day, minus ten minutes for his bath and shampoo. Bless his heart, he never once complained about it from the minute I put it on him. He just looked at me as if to say, "If Mama says so, it must be so." When he went to bed with that cumbersome thing on his head, he simply closed his eyes and went to sleep. It was never an issue, and sure enough, as the doctor predicted, six months later he no longer needed to wear it. I was so proud of him.

Diego was such a joy in my life. He was magical, he was effervescent. He was also going to be a big brother. The call came, Mary, will you take this baby? Diego's birth mother delivered a baby girl, Gabriela, also going through heroin withdrawals, and she too needed a home. As far as I was concerned she was already family and I couldn't wait to meet her.

When a baby tests positive for illegal drugs, of any kind, at birth, they are always placed in protective care.

Gabriela was all of six pounds and looked like her brother. The same dark hair sticking straight up, and captivating eyes as big as saucers. I was thrilled she didn't present with his piercing newborn scream! We were a family for however long they needed me, and if she was anything like Diego, I was prepared to hold on for the ride.

Several times over the course of Diego's stay with me, I took short term emergency placements, so he grew used to seeing little babies coming and going. He never paid much attention, of course his cars and trucks were his preoccupation.

What I was not expecting was his reaction to THIS baby. He couldn't seem to get enough of her, never letting her out of his sight till lights out every night. He was the proverbial mother hen. It was clear she wouldn't be needing me for much as long as she had her big brother. I marveled at their instant connection. Diego was so loving, and she so accepting of his attention. If she fussed the least bit he'd run to her side and she'd stop right away. There were times when her withdrawal tremors were extremely bad and Diego would sit beside us, stroking her arm as together we calmed her. If I asked him to give her *a lovey*, he'd ever so gently lay his head on her chest and close his eyes.

It wasn't long before he decided it was his job to feed her as well. With a toy car in one hand, her bottle in the other, and that ever present smile, he'd stand over her until she'd taken the last drop. I'm sure if he could have bumped her, he'd have done that as well. Diapering was another aspect of her care he wanted to oversee. I'd lay her on the changing table, he'd climb up the side to supervise. They just seemed to know they were brother and sister, together all the time. Diego now had two passions in his life, his cars and his Gabriela. It did my heart good.

You may wonder why I didn't adopt *all* my little angels; I'm often asked that question. Well, many of them came while I was raising my daughter and son. After they were grown and out on their own, I was too tired to go back to grade school, PTA meetings, learning to drive, and the dating scene. My babies needed young parents who could keep up with them, be there for the long haul. Anything short of that wouldn't have been in their best interest, and too, I've never seen an orphanage up for sale! Diego was

64

nearing seventeen months old, Gabriela near three months, when another family wanted to meet him. I sometimes wondered what went through the minds of people looking to adopt. Did they have a preconceived notion as to what their new son or daughter should look like? Did they want a certain stature, eye color, or skin color? Would they know he or she was the one for them as soon as they locked eyes? What would be the deciding factor? A smile, their cleverness, or something as special as *making flirty eyes!* I worried, if only *one* was a perfect match, how would they handle being split up.

The day of the visit I arranged for a friend to watch Gabriela so as not to steal Diego's thunder. As visits go, and I'd seen many over the years, this one was incredible. There was no awkwardness, uneasiness, or nerves getting in the way. We were all having a good time.

As I had wondered about first visits, I also wondered what the families thoughts must have been as they drove away after. There was so much to consider, and such a monumental commitment to be made.

Two weeks later another visit was scheduled, Diego had just turned eighteen months old. A decision had been reached, he was going to have his own forever family, and, they were considering adopting Gabriela as well once she was free for adoption. If I had to let them go, this was the family I knew would love, nurture, and keep them safe.

The day Diego left I held him in my arms and together we released eighteen balloons, one for every month he was part of my life. Then I kissed him goodbye.

That evening, as I fed Gabriela, my tears rolled down the side of her bottle. There were no cars tucked between the folds of her blanket, and later, no little eyes gazed through the slats of her crib as if to say "night night" as she drifted off to sleep. Her brother was gone.

In the weeks that followed we stayed busy and on the go. She was still young enough that, though I'm sure she missed him, she didn't know how to show it. I worried it would be hardest on Diego. I came up with a plan.

I bought some poster board, a few big markers, and got out my camera. I put a message on the poster board, "Hi Diego, this is me eating my first real food," and took a picture of her beside it. Others read, "I can sit up now, and I like cars too." In the shots she was surrounded by cars. I mailed them to Diego so he could see everything she was learning to do, and hopefully still feel their special connection.

Gabriela stayed with me for almost a year before she was free for adoption, then joined her big brother, *forever*. They are happy, thriving, and as close as ever. Diego is full of mischief and quiet, reserved Gabriela follows his lead. Case in point; they learned to print their names but used the bedroom walls as paper. Daddy calmly sat them down and explained they must never again write on the walls. Next day, upon returning from work, their names were prominently displayed across the front of the house and deck. Daddy corralled the pair of them, repeated their last conversation and stressed, *no writing on any walls what so ever!!*

He then gave them each a bucket of warm soapy water to remove the evidence of their misadventure. The following day Daddy received a call at work from mom, who was trying to disguise her laughter. Within the hour, as Daddy pulled into the driveway, Diego and Gabriela were standing by the door, their names written all over their arms and legs! Diego had the biggest grin on his face, and as their mom related to me, Gabriela looked scared to death. Diego was quick to chime in with, "No one said we couldn't write on ourselves!!"

Hannah

The Circle of Love

I met Hannah in a detox facility for infants, she was three months old and going through severe withdrawals. She'd been *swimming* in opiates from conception, and needed to be on drugs to safely come off drugs. If you've ever watched a program depicting adults going through withdrawals, you'll know how shocking it is to watch. To hold, and try to comfort a five pound baby going through the same nightmare, is nothing short of horrific as they're weaned off their mother's drugs, and their cravings subside. That's what Hannah was going through.

I stood gazing over her crib as she lay swaddled and sleeping. Her room was sparse and pristine, even the floor sparkled. As I looked around I thought, this isn't the way it's supposed to be, and what a sad introduction to the world. There were no fairy-tail pictures hanging on the walls, no frilly curtains, just plain white wooden blinds. No fluffy stuffed animals, and no mobiles circling overhead playing lullabies. The word austere came to mind. What bothered me most was no mommy hovering over her tiny trembling body humming long remembered childhood tunes.

The majority of my babies were drug-exposed, but not all to the same extent. How each went through withdrawals was dependent upon the specific drugs their mother used, and how often. Each one presented with different reactions. Some could be managed in my home without medications. Very often they'd sleep around the clock, not waking to eat, thus at greater risk of weight loss and failure to thrive. They'd have to be awakened and fed on a strict schedule. By comparison, some demonstrated ungovernable frenzied screams that brought tears to my eyes; it was that hard to watch. Some presented with increased, or no muscle tone. It was common to see their tiny bodies shaking violently craving the addictive substances they had ingested in utero. Still others broke out in cold sweats, some developed respiratory issues, and many had repeated seizures.

Tiny Hannah was having a particularly difficult time, and to make matters worse, she developed Methicillin Resistant Staphylococcus Aureus, MRSA, a life-threatening contagious infection. The state called, "Mary, will you take *this* baby?" To be truthful, I was more than a little hesitant. I needed to do some research before committing myself and taking such a high risk. I made an appointment with the head of communicable diseases at my local hospital. I contacted the Department of Health, and spoke with the Center For Disease Control (CDC). What I learned was jaw dropping and eye opening, but I could only deal with what I understood. I agreed to take her. MRSA could be spread just like a cold, and live on surfaces for months. Hannah's lesions were on the side of her face; pus-filled blisters that had to be drained and the fluid cultured.

She was on an oral antibiotic, and I had to apply an antibiotic cream over the lesions three times a day. I learned she'd been through a previous battle with MRSA in her first weeks of life. Some people can be carriers. They have it on their skin and in their nose, though they show no symptoms, making it especially dangerous and easy to come in contact with.

Hannah needed a quiet environment, low stimulation, and special handling. Hospital staff taught me specific ways to hold her, curled against my body while facing a blank wall, and how to rock her. Not just side to side as all mothers instinctively do, but head to toe as well. I learned how to put pressure on her head and back to calm her when her cravings caused her to lose control. Every aspect of her care was centered around *what* and *how much* stimuli she could tolerate, I had to be the judge. I learned to read her cues by trial and error.

Because of past concerns with my babies, I made a point to ask if Hannah had been tested for HIV; she had not. Her birth mother had no pre-natal care throughout her pregnancy, so the option of being tested herself was never brought up. That being said, coupled with the drug exposure, and mom's dangerous lifestyle while she was in utero, Hannah could not have been more at risk for HIV. I'd been down this road before, surely this time it would be different and they'd test her. Instead, nothing had changed. Because foster parents are not legal guardians, the authority to test lies with the state and they weren't required to take action simply because I asked. The all-too-familiar brick walls were looming before me.

The day after bringing her home we met with the pediatrician to have the MRSA checked. Again I asked about having her tested for HIV. This doctor felt it was in her best interest and prepared the lab request. But if wasn't that easy. I still needed a court order. Every time I spoke with the social worker I asked about having the test done. I went up and down the chain of command to no avail. I went to her supervisor, the guardian ad litem, explaining that the longer intervention was delayed, the less hopeful it was that HIV could be eradicated *if* it was in her system. Without the court order, my hands were tied.

At home I made sure her nursery was outfitted similar to the one she left in the detox center. Everything was white and plain with minimal decorations and accessories. It made the transition easier on her. My house was quiet, and at first I kept her only in the nursery until she adjusted to me, my voice, and my touch. I had to be most vigilant when I was feeding her. The least bit or over stimulation and she'd quit sucking, become frantic, and lose control. It could take thirty minutes or more to get her back on track. Once she was calm around me, and eating well, we ventured downstairs to more color, sounds, and space. Everything was introduced a little at a time and she did well.

I was becoming more comfortable dealing with the residual effects of her drug exposure, but the MRSA was a different matter entirely. Though I knew what to do, I worried I too would become infected. I had to find that part of myself, again, that would help me see past my fear.

I wore rubber gloves every time I was near the infection site, and disinfected the tub following ever bath. Her clothing, bedding, towels, and wash clothes had to be washed separately. For a while I thought I'd wash the skin right off my hands; I was that scared. Her bottles and nipples had to be sterilized and stored away from other dishes. Hannah needed my help, and I sure as hell wasn't going to let her down.

I'm an avid runner and walker, so sooner or later all my little charges were introduced to what I called, "squeals on wheels." They loved a fast buggy ride down the road, the faster the better till I was near exhaustion. Now it was Hannah's turn to feel the exhilaration. I wasn't prepared for her reaction.

Having never been outside before, other than two short car rides, the trees along the road sent her into an absolute meltdown. She was over-stimulated. I should have realized this could happen. I was mindful of her environment in my home, but didn't think something we all take for granted, a tree, could be too overwhelming for her. The following day I started with five minutes standing by a large window, then in the doorway. After a few more days, we were in the yard surrounded by several very large trees with no adverse reaction. Daily walks were part of our day from then on.

She had a similar reaction the first time I took her to the mall. So many people, loud voices, and movement all around. This time I had a plan. I covered all but a small opening on the hood of the buggy. She could still see out, but only a little at a time. Each trip I made the opening a little bigger, until eventually no cover was needed. She was doing great, becoming content and accepting of the world around her.

Hannah was a sweetheart. She loved to be cuddled and just talked to. She wasn't even a year old, and we'd already discussed dating, college, and the facts of life. She knew what was expected of her, I could only hope it sunk in even at her tender young age. I always introduced my babies to classical music; Hannah was no exception. It had a calming effect on all of them, and I seldom had difficulty getting them to sleep if Pavarotti was belting out a passionate aria in the background.

She was eating well, responsive, and engaging. Her MRSA was clearing up, she was progressing in all developmental areas, and meeting the usual infant milestones. Most important of all, she knew she was loved.

Behind the scenes, the stress relating to her care was beginning to show on me. I had been dealing with the MRSA, the possibility she could have HIV, as well as not being out of rehab long. Added to that, I was still unable to get the court order needed to have her tested for HIV. I was continually dealing with state officials. I realized I could no longer care for the babies, at the same time fight *the system* for what they needed. After much soul-searching, anguish, and tearful, sleepless nights, I closed my license. Hannah was moved to another foster home.

That day I looked at myself from a different perspective; I was no longer a foster mother. I looked at the photos of my babies, the newspaper articles, and the award on the wall. It all reflected the life that defined who I was for so many years. I knew I made a difference, I did the best I could, but was it enough? Did I let the system get the better of me, did I let my babies down?

The way I see it, Hannah, and all the other babies in the system, then and now, have rights, *most importantly the right to live.* As with all the other pokes and jabs our babies get to protect them, so it should be with an HIV test, if the doctor feels it's warranted. Two pediatricians recommended she be tested; it made no difference. My precious Hannah had already been through hell and back. Without testing I feared she'd have to go through yet another hell in the years ahead, and not come back. That's how HIV/AIDS works.

She was the last baby to leave my home. I never heard anything more about her as if she'd fallen from the face of the earth. My heart was broken. I missed her dearly, and the thought of no more babies to love and watch over, was almost too much to bear.

Both nurseries remained ready to use for eight more months. I couldn't explain why at the time. Every day I just needed to go in and look around, remembering tiny faces from the past. In retrospect I think it took me that long to come to terms with the ending, then I was ready to let go, for the last time.

A truck parked in my driveway and by days end, all my baby things were gone. The nurseries were empty, the garage was empty, and after three decades of counting little toes, I felt empty as well. My job was to love them, keep them safe, get them healthy, then let go. I knew that right up front. No one said it would be easy, but there are no words to adequately describe the rewards. Now at age sixty-four, it's been a whole new experience re-learning how to walk upright without a buggy, use stairs instead of elevators, and carry a purse instead of a diaper bag.

I hadn't forgotten my whispered promise to baby Claire. To that end, I went back to the legislature with renewed determination to keep fighting for the babies. My journey wasn't over yet.

"We can do no great things. Just small things, with great love."
—Mother Teresa 1910-1997

If you'd like to become a foster parent, you can contact DSHS, the Department of Social and Health Services in your area.

PART III

MY PROMISE

Dedicated To Baby Sue

A moment of time in my life, till the end of time in my heart.
—It was 2003

You know all is right in the world when you hold a new baby in your arms, gaze into their eyes, and your hearts beat as one. That's the way it's supposed to be. I felt that special bond more often than most as a foster mother for infants in the care of the State, spanning three decades. But it all changed with baby Sue.

I was so excited when each baby came into my life, as if they were my own. Some were only hours old when I picked them up at the hospital, some were delivered to my door, and others I got to know over several weeks while still in the hospital waiting to be well enough for me to take home. Hospital staff trained me to take care of their special needs. Once in my care, it was routine to see health care vans dropping off various pieces of equipment, including oxygen tanks as tall, and as big around as myself, nor was it uncommon to see fire trucks and ambulances pulling up to my front door lights flashing, and sirens blaring.

My babies needed care, but they also needed socialization, and a smile on their face. That meant being out and about with a couple of monitors, portable oxygen canisters, feeding tubes, and diaper bag all in tow.

Some stayed with me a day, a couple of months, even a few years. The usual was about eighteen months. It didn't matter how long; they all brought joy into my life, and I learned so much from each one. They showed me what I was capable of, and I drew strength from their strength. They were a constant reminder of my own many blessings.

For awhile I did emergency placements as well as regular foster care. I had two nurseries set up, licensed to care for two babies at a time. On occasion, police officers would bring me a baby in the middle of the night. Some from domestic violence situations, some from the back seat of parked cars behind taverns. That was, and still is the nature of foster parenting. Heartbreaking, but always rewarding.

* * *

Two week old Sue had blonde hair, blue eyes, and skin that shone like porcelain. At first glance, she appeared calm, with her tiny thumb tucked between her lips. But I had been forewarned; there was another side to Sue. Her quiet times were few and far between; she was addicted to methamphetamines.

Often, babies in her condition require a doctor's supervision in a rehab facility, while on drugs, to come off drugs. Her pediatrician felt an experienced caregiver, in a home environment, would be in Sue's best interest. I agreed to take her.

She was the first little girl I'd had in a long time. I'd get to use the basket full of brightly colored ribbons for her hair, as well as the little smocked dresses hanging in the closet. It would take awhile to meet the real Sue though, once the drugs were out of her system.

How a newborn goes through withdrawals is dependent upon what the mother used, and how often. Each one presents with different reactions, all gut-wrenching and shocking to have to watch, as their tiny bodies convulse violently, craving the addictive substance they'd been getting in the months prior to birth. For Sue it was no different. I'd been down this road before, more times than I cared to remember. I knew full well I had to be strong for her. We'd get through it together.

By two months old the lingering effects of the meth, fitful screaming nights, tremors, and poor eating were lessening, and a delightful personality was emerging. She was happy, engaging, and beginning to meet the usual infant milestones. Just when I thought she was out-of-the-woods, her

doctor suspected something was wrong with her left eye. A specialist at Children's Hospital confirmed her suspicions; there was no optic nerve; the eye was blind.

What did life have in store for this precious little girl who'd been removed from her birth mother, for her own safety, fought her way through hor-rendous withdrawals, and was blind in one eye? It wasn't the way her life should have begun.

As the weeks went by, signs of failure to thrive dissipated. Sue had more fire in her than I'd seen in a baby for a long time. It was pure joy to watch the little dynamo in action. For sure one eye wasn't going to slow her down. I was so proud of her.

She wasn't the only baby in my home. I had one-year-old Joey who was developmentally disabled and needed around-the-clock supervision. Before long Sue took it upon herself to be his shadow, his buddy and his," Little

Mommy." It was as if she knew instinctively Joey was different and needed her help. They were inseparable and soon became ingrained in my heart and soul, though I hesitate to add, an hour of listening to Sue blowing on her harmonica could get a little testy at times, especially when hubby joined in with his harmonica. In retrospect, I think I had three babies in the house. Life was good. I made a point to take each day in stride and make life as normal as possible for the babies whose lives were anything but.

As this was playing out, a family came forward interested in meeting Sue with the intent to adopt. She was at that adorable stage of unsure, wobbly first steps, learning to talk, and giggled, it seemed, at everything. How could they not fall in love with her? Several home visits were set up as the adoption paperwork moved forward. Sue was inching her way closer to having a forever family. Everyone was happy, until we got the call. "We believe Sue is HIV positive."

* * *

The line seemed to go dead; the silence was deafening. I couldn't speak. In that instant my world dropped out from under me. All I could think about was Sue and my family. I felt panic engulf me as I struggled for words that wouldn't come. The social worker told me she'd arrange for a court order to

have the test done and drop it by the house the next day. I don't remember hanging up. I wanted to cry; I wanted to run; I wanted to forget the phone conversation. But most of all I wanted to scream.

I didn't know much about HIV other than what I'd heard on television and read in newspapers. It was frightening. I got no sleep that night. The test was scheduled for 3:30 the next day. Another hurdle for Sue to get over loomed on the horizon. I knew then all was not right in the world.

It was like any other blood draw. Bless her heart, she lay in my arms sucking her thumb, oblivious to the importance of one small tube of blood. She didn't even cry. I was astonished when the nurse asked me to hold a piece of gauze over the still bleeding draw site. I looked her straight in the eyes and said, "You're testing for HIV, you're the one wearing gloves."

There are no words to describe how we got through the next three days waiting for the test results to come back. It was 2003. Today the same results would be back within minutes. I tried to stay busy, visited all the local parks, walked miles around the mall, and scrubbed every floor in the house. I had seventy-two hours to worry myself to death.

I thought about Sue, when she cracked the television control guard in an attempt to push the buttons. She nicked the tip of her finger twice trying. Each time I just wiped the blood away thinking nothing of it. I thought about Joey, and how the two of them shared everything, toys, spoons, even their cheerios. I thought about the doctor who operated on her eye; he could have been infected as well. How could this have happened? I vacillated between being scared, and being angry.

Those three days dragged on for what seemed an eternity. Finally, the test results were back. Sue did not have HIV.

Life returned to what I can only describe as a guarded normal. Our joy and laughter after the scare

was short lived, the adoption was only weeks away.

I was happy for Sue when the big day came. I liked her new Mom and Dad, and her new big sister.

Now she had her forever family, what I consider to be life's greatest gift. Knowing that made it easier to let go. As I kissed her goodbye, I held her close, told her how much I loved her, and whispered a promise in her ear.

* * *

Oh, how I missed her as the days and weeks went by. I longed to hear the harmonica, and wondered, when she called "Mama," did she go looking for me as she always did? I questioned if I could continue as a foster mother.

My anger kept coming back. How could this, "thing" called HIV have touched my world? I thought it only happened to others, continents away, not here in my small town, in my sweet innocent little baby. The more I thought about it, the more I wanted to know, the more I had to know. I set out to educate myself.

When a baby's born, the mother passes her antibodies to the child. In simple terms, those antibodies

circulate in the baby for about six months, ideally protecting it's health until they've stored antibodies of their own, then the mother's dissipate. In the same way, if the mother does have HIV, it's passed to her baby through her antibodies.

HIV attacks the body's immune system, destroying cells that help fight disease. Left undetected it leads to AIDS, Acquired Immune Deficiency Syndrome. Treatment can reduce the amount of HIV in your blood, called viral load, increase the good cells and increase the body's ability to ward off disease. Babies born to HIV infected Moms, receive Zidovudine for six weeks following birth and are tested twice before a positive or negative diagnosis is given. There's a window of opportunity when, if treated, the virus can be stopped before it settles in a baby's body to stay. That window starts during labor, and within twelve hours following delivery.

Sue's mother was known to have an addiction to meth, lived a reckless and dangerous life style,

putting her baby at great risk. The State also put Sue at risk knowing she too was addicted, and not having her tested for HIV at birth. I was horrified to learn the State was aware of the possibility of her

having the virus soon after she was born, but kept it under wraps until her adoption was ready to go

forward. By allowing this cloak of secrecy, under the guise of privacy, was a form of child abuse, as far as I was concerned. A representative for the State later told a reporter, that not telling me up front that Sue may have been HIV positive was an, "oversight." In my mind, it was incomprehensible, and became a major turning point for me.

I was a firm believer that in taking these adorable, sweet, infants into my home, and my life, I was in for the long haul, whatever it took to make their lives better, and whatever it took to keep them safe. My babies had no voice. I did. If I had to shout, I would do that too.

I had to do something before another child, and another foster family suffered as we did. But where would I start? I was, "just a Mom." *"The most difficult thing is the decision to act. The rest is merely tenacity."

* * *

Well, I started in the wrong place. Having little real knowledge about how laws are created, changed, or enacted, I went to my local newspaper thinking I'd find a lead there, but no such luck. Driving through town that afternoon, I was stopped in traffic in front of an impressive high-rise bearing a name of it's own...The Norm Dick's Government Center. I'd heard his name mentioned before, linked to some powerful undertakings and figured he must

81

carry some clout to warrant his own building. He might be just the person I needed to talk to. What did I have to lose.

I got out my not so impressive looking, faux parchment, yellow, legal pad, and began to write, laying my concerns on the table. I told him I wanted all babies, one year of age and under in the custody of the state, and subsequently placed in foster care, who's birth mother's HIV status was unknown, to be tested for the HIV virus and Hepatitis C. I wanted the test results made known to foster parents at time of placement. I addressed it and mailed it as fast as I could so as not to lose my momentum or nerve. I worried; had I sounded too forward in my choice of words, too demanding maybe, and would I even get a reply?

Wednesday, the following week, a very official looking envelope with blue lettering and the words,

"Congress of the United States" arrived in the mail, my mail! I couldn't believe it. My hands were shaking as I stood staring at it, afraid to open it at first. It read in part ...

"Although I would appreciate this opportunity to assist you with your request, regrettably, I am unable to serve you since your concern is a state issue which is outside of my federal jurisdiction. I am respectfully referring your request to Senator Betti Sheldon in Olympia," signed Norm Dicks, Member of Congress.

* * *

I had started the ball rolling. It was 2003. In between changing diapers and 2:00 AM feedings, I made time to do a bit of research, starting with the Washington State Constitution, Article 1, Section 1.

"All political power is inherent in the people, and governments derive their just powers from the consent of the governed, and are established to protect and maintain individual rights."

It also states:

"Every person may freely speak, write, and publish on all subjects, being responsible for the abuse of that right."

These two excerpts kept coming to mind. All political power it said, and protecting individual rights. What was I getting myself into? Then I remembered, "I was in for the long haul, whatever it took to make their lives better, whatever it took to keep them safe." It wasn't scary anymore, now I felt empowered.

* * *

By October of that year, I was meeting with Senator Sheldon, and Representative Rockefeller, discussing how to proceed. They agreed with me; simply taking precautions around human blood and body fluids was not enough. Policy and practice needed to be revised. We discussed the fact that discovery of a newborn's HIV status would automatically disclose the status of the mother. A few states were being challenged in court based on the argument that it violated a mother's constitutional right to privacy. A law requiring the same testing in our state would very likely be challenged as well. However, since foster children are in the custody of the state, not the biological mother, it offered a plausible loop hole to proceed with legislation. The complexity of the issue, including legal ramifications, would make it a difficult matter to address, but one that warranted further attention. They were on board. We were talking the same language though they made it clear we had our work cut out for us. Representative Rockefeller took the lead and agreed to introduce a bill on my behalf. He asked if he could count on me to testify.

On January 19, 2004, House Bill (HB) 2699 was introduced in the Legislature. Unfortunately, it didn't receive a hearing in Committee by the cut-off date, and was classified a "dead bill," not to be considered further that session.

It was devastating news, the wind knocked out of me. This was going to be harder than I thought. It was stupid of me to take on such a huge undertaking without being more informed. I had only myself to blame for the way I felt when I hit the first of many stumbling blocks to come. I'd have to learn how to circumvent the bumps in the road, learn more about what I was doing, and what I was up against. It wouldn't be the first, nor the last time, when I'd learn a valuable lesson. It all came down to doing some leg work, and some homework. I had my work cut out for me.

* * *

A bill is introduced in either the Senate or House of Representatives by a member. It is then referred to a committee hearing, who study the content, and hold public hearings. They have the option to pass, reject, or take no action. If it's passed in committee, it's then read in open session of the House or Senate, called the first reading, then passed to the Rules Committee. They can place the bill on second reading for debate before the entire body or take no action. If the bill makes it this far, it's subject to further debate before being placed on third reading for final passage. All bills must have three readings in both the House and the Senate in order to pass the Legislature. If amendments are made, the other house must approve the changes, then it's signed by the respective leaders and forwarded to the Governor. He can veto the entire bill, parts of the bill, or sign it into law.

In odd-numbered years, when the budget is being debated, session lasts 105 days, in even-numbered years, sixty days. During that short period of time, legislators deal with the introduction of thousands of bills. They cast votes on hundreds, and can't possibly keep track of the intricate details of each one. Lobbyists vie for their time, attention, and votes, as well as the thousands of constituents in their districts wanting to be heard. In the midst of the fray was me, little insignificant me saying, "I'd like this made law, now ... please."

It was disheartening that HB 2699 was short lived, but Representative Rockefeller and I were determined to follow through. There would be no turning back if I had anything to do with it.

I learned two things over the course of that Legislative session. First, I had nothing to fear and so much to gain. Second, though the process of getting a bill passed seemed daunting at first, I understood the relevancy of it all, and dug my heels in further. My determination and strength were rooted in one little girl, and one big promise.

* * *

I was still, just a Mom, but had taken on a new title, Advocate. Advocacy means to speak up, to plead the case of another, or to champion a cause. It represents the best hope for disclosing why there's a problem in the first place. Some advocacy is done by experts called Lobbyists. I was nowhere near that level. I simply cared enough to get involved, to speak up for Sue, and all the other foster babies. I wanted government policies to work for the most vulnerable, as well as they did for the most powerful.

If I was going to carry the title I had to learn how to do the best I could. I joined CWAC, the Child Welfare Advocacy Coalition. They work in conjunction with the Legislature to ensure children in the welfare system receive appropriate and quality care. It meant a two hour trek, every Friday morning, while session was in, for a one hour meeting, with baby, bottles, and buggy in tow. I was the only one there with an infant, but more-often-than-not, they slept through the meetings as long as they were dry and well fed. While they snoozed, we discussed the bills pertaining to children and how we could effect a positive outcome. I learned a lot about how dedicated individuals come together with the sole

objective of looking out for the future of the tiniest and most deserving. I always looked forward to those Friday mornings. They inspired me and gave me great purpose.

* * *

So we had a small set-back with HB 2699. I decided I'd get more involved the next time, put my best-self out there, change my image, and my approach, in order to make people take notice and garner the support I needed. Instead of the low keyed, soft spoken Mary I was at home, singing lullabies and changing diapers, I wanted to be seen and heard for who I was when it came to fighting for the babies I loved.

The next time I was on the legislative campus, following a meeting with Representative Rockefeller, I sat on a bench outside his office, and took in my surroundings, watching and listening, taking mental notes. I saw a plethora of steps, an abundance of marble, men and women in dark, tailored suits coming and going at an alarming pace, with briefcases in one hand, lattes or phones in the other. There sat me in my mundane, beige, understated Ralph Lauren dress slacks, brown long sleeve sweater and, "comfortable" walking shoes. No doubt I stuck out in the crowd, but for all the wrong reasons. I needed to look like I was there on a mission and knew what I was talking about.

I drove home and ferreted out my best black suit. My comfortable shoes were replaced with

four inch pointed toe high heels, and a trip to the mall produced the perfect briefcase. I put it all together, looked in the mirror and thought, yes, now you look like a woman who means business.

* * *

HB 3081 was introduced. Basically it said the same as HB 2699. "The Legislature intends to establish a policy with the goal of ensuring the health and well-being of both infants in foster care, and the families providing their care." It was first read on January 19, 2004 and referred to the Committee on Children and Family Services. I was going to testify for the first time.

Legislative hearings are conducted informally. They're not judicial proceedings and are somewhat relaxed. Anyone can testify, no formal training is required, and I was told not to be nervous or worried, which, as we all know means, it's time to worry!

As it happened, on that day I had a new foster baby with me as well as my husband. Christopher was only five days old. Representative Rockefeller introduced all three of us, and remarked that baby Christopher was the youngest young man ever to show up for a committee hearing.

They called my name and I started down the isle. The room was packed. Eight State Representatives seated in a tiered semi-circle in front of me became a blur as I took my seat and reached for the microphone. I began to shake; all eyes were on me. I could feel the blood draining from my head as I struggled to keep my composure. The room went silent. I had something important to say and I damn sure wasn't going to miss the opportunity. It was all up to me, I couldn't mess it up now. I looked down at the photo of Sue I held tight in the palm of my hand, and remembered why I was there, not who was there. Everything came back into focus. I opened my mouth and began, "Madame Chair, members of the Committee . . ."

I made it clear why I wanted HB 3081 passed into law, and ended by saying,

87

"On December 1st, I picked up a newborn baby at the hospital, both he and his mother tested positive for drugs when he was born. Now I'm scared, now I need assurances. Please don't let this happen to another child or foster family. I feel there is a growing lack of awareness, certainly complacency towards the gravity of blood-borne pathogens in our community. Unless it touches their family, the general public doesn't give it much thought. For three days it touched my family profoundly. The way policy stands now, every time I pick up a new baby I must ask myself, do I feel lucky?

If babies are tested it becomes a win-win solution both for the baby's health care, and that of the foster parent's. There aren't enough foster parents now to fill the need. If no one will fight for our safety, who will bring the babies home? Who will turn on the porch light for a police officer dropping

off an infant in the middle of the night? The cliché, what you don't know won't hurt you, becomes, what you don't know may kill you."

Being able to address the committee reaffirmed my commitment to the babies. I'd had my say, it was invigorating, and I felt strong. The bill was in their hands now.

* * *

As Donald and I and baby Christopher prepared to leave for home, the skies opened up, and a torrential downpour unleashed its fury on us halfway to the parking lot. Baby and I took shelter in the nearest doorway while Donald ran for the car. On his return, as we hastened to get out of the deluge, neither of us noticed posted signs in front of the building. A police cruiser pulled alongside, lights flashing, and a big burly officer approached. He wanted to know who we were, and why we were parked in Governor Locke's parking space! Embarrassed, we explained everything, apologized profusely, and he told us not to hurry, "Take good care of the little one, and be on your way." I'd had more than enough excitement for one day having just given my first testimony, then the encounter with campus police. I couldn't wait to get home, back to what I knew best, taking care of babies.

* * *

HB3081 passed into law as a Substitute House Bill (SHB 3081) that session; a watered down version of what I initially asked for. The fact that it passed was overshadowed by the changes made, and presented another stumbling block to get around. At least it piqued enough interest to warrant a closer look.

Representative Rockefeller warned me that, because of the complexity of the bill, including legal issues, test protocols, and reliability, any legislation to address my concerns would be of interest to many, but not all would necessarily agree with one another as to the best course of action to take.

The revised bill required the Department of Health (DOH), to develop recommendations for evidence-based practices, focusing on mandatory testing for blood-borne pathogens. Blood-borne

pathogens are microorganisms present in blood that can cause disease and death in humans. HIV was central to that train of thought. On completion, they had to report their recommendations back to the Legislature by January 1st the following year, just prior to the start of the next session. If the report came back in my favor, we'd have time to squeeze in a new bill, if it didn't, I'd be back at the drawing board... for another year. Somehow, fingers crossed didn't seem enough.

* * *

To do the study, they convened a panel of eight experts from across the state, as well as five DOH staff support members, at some expense to taxpayers, I'm sure. The panel was comprised of four doctors, the Foster Care Health Issues Program Manager, two registered nurses, and the Public Policy Director of Children's Home Society in Washington. The substitute bill defined the process and information to be considered in developing the department's conclusions and recommendations. In short, their primary objective was to identify the specific pathogens for which testing was recommended. I thought, okay, this might take awhile, but I'm sure they'll come around. I couldn't see any other outcome. We were talking about a life or death decision, we were talking about babies, and as far as I was concerned, we were talking about a lifetime, the one every baby deserves.

Thirteen agents defined as blood-borne pathogens that could be transmitted from mother to child during gestation or child birth were to be studied. Of those, nine were singled out, found to be very rare in the United States, and unlikely to be missed in a pregnant woman or newborn. For that reason, they were no longer considered part of the study. A more detailed analysis and discussion concerning the four remaining blood-borne pathogens became the focus of their attention. They were HIV, hepatitis B, hepatitis C, and syphilis. All hepatitis attacks the liver, it's an inflammation that can progress to cirrhosis, scarring, and cancer. A virus is the most common cause, but alcohol, drugs and auto-immune diseases can also cause it. There are five hepatitis viruses of which, Hep B, C and D, usually occur as a result of contact with infected body fluids. You can also get hepatitis from contaminated blood, invasive medical procedures, and non sterile equipment.

Syphilis is a sexually transmitted, highly contagious disease that can have serious complications. When left untreated in adults, it can cause brain damage and blindness. Transmission from mother to child can cause abnormalities, even death. When I married in 1970, no one could get a marriage license without first being tested for syphilis. As a result the disease was almost obliterated. Why was testing for HIV treated any different?

For nine long months I bided my time waiting for the DOH conclusions. A pattern was developing, hurry up and wait. It was a good thing I had my babies to divert my attention. There never seemed enough hours in a day to finish my to-do lists. What with doctor's appointments near and far, physical therapy sessions for some, administering and monitoring their often long list of medications; there was little time for anything else. I loved the early evening hours best. I was in for the night, could sit back and enjoy my babies, putting the demands of the next day out of my head. I cherished those moments, a bit of quiet in the turmoil surrounding me. Finally the results were back. The report read, Identification of the specific pathogens, for which testing is recommended . . . HIV.

It was the only one. The panel also recommended the Department of Social and Health Services, (DSHS) re-examine their current policies and practices regarding HIV testing of infants, for which they already had authority to make medical decisions. It was more than I could have hoped for. I did it, I did it, was my first thought, but my excitement was premature, the wind sucked from my sails . . . again.

* * *

Though the report said, do this, in subsequent weeks there was no effort made by the Legislature to get enabling legislation. Were they waiting for my next move? Did they doubt my tenacity? Did they think I'd go away? Even more disheartening, in an interview with the press, now Senator Rockefeller, said the issue of testing was considered, but the Legislature was, "Not prepared to tell doctors how to carry out their professional duties. They are encouraged to test," he said, "but to mandate testing would be a burden on the whole system." He concluded by saying, "I think we arrived at the best we could get." Everything came to a standstill. I felt like I'd been hit in the gut. I couldn't understand the sudden shift in direction. The bill was losing what little momentum it had. I began to fear the worst and it didn't look good. I was back to square one. Everything shouted, "Walk away Mary, you did your best, walk away."

* * *

Remember baby Sue, the precious little girl who started me on this journey? Well, I received a call from the state, "Mary, will you take this baby?" Sue had a new baby sister who was also at high risk for HIV. I agreed to take her. How could I not, she was Sue's sister, as far as I was concerned, she was family. When I asked for a court order to have her tested, I got the same response, no response. If she was HIV positive, by now she was past the window of time when antiretroviral drug therapy could have saved her life.

* * *

With the return of the DOH study, and write-up in the local newspaper, Representative Sherry Appleton, 23rd district, came forward. She felt otherwise about the whole testing issue, thought lawmakers should have followed through on the recommendations, and was prepared to introduce a new bill the next session. In her words, "If you have a report that says, this should be done, then the next logical step is that it gets done." It wasn't long after, a letter arrived from Representative Appleton's aide asking what I thought about the recent turn of events regarding HB 3081. I got out my trusty pen.

| *Donna,*

"My stand remains the same, drug positive babies should automatically be tested for HIV. When a baby tests positive for drugs, in affect DSHS says, sorry Mom, you aren't responsible enough to care for your baby so he/she is going into foster care, done. Now the state is in control, but they drop the ball because the baby can be carrying the HIV virus, and can infect others. Testing could prevent the baby from ever coming down with AIDS. A $6.00 blood test can protect the foster home, other foster children in the home, and most important, save the child. The big issue seems to be rights and privacy.

Who's rights? I feel the baby's right to a long and healthy life far out-weights that of the birth mother, who is addicted to drugs, and already judged not fit to care for her baby.

HIV issues may not surface very often in our area, but understand this; they surfaced in my home, in my life, and, "we're sorry" will never take away the fear and anguish we went through.

The Department of Social and Health Services say they will tell me when a child is HIV positive, "if known." What good does that do me? They need to test in order to "make known" a child's status. Disclosure will also give me the choice of caring for an HIV infected baby. I have that right, but in so doing, I feel the state fears losing licensed homes.

The pandemic of HIV/AIDS in the world did not start with a massive out-break, rather one case at a time. Is that what I'm up against with each baby I take into my home?

Information you sent me says Children's Administration has policies and procedures in place to address the panel's recommendations regarding training. We must be interpreting the panel's report quite differently. I read it as saying, very clearly, IDENTIFICATION OF THE SPECIFIC PATHOGEN FOR WHICH TESTING IS RECOMMENDED, HIV. DSHS keeps going on about training, training, training, rights, and privacy, thus evading the real issue of testing.

To address Children's Administration's Case Service Manual, Foster Parent's Rights; we have the right to voice grievances about treatment furnished, or, not furnished to a foster child. That's what I'm doing.

I've been to support groups for foster parents. They, as well as adoptive parents, tell me how frightened they are of HIV. I speak from both camps.

Is testing really too much to ask? It will only take one time, when a child isn't tested, is positive, and a family is forever changed.

My babies are my life, there isn't anything I wouldn't do for them. We must look out for these most precious of all beings."

Representative Appleton's "people" asked for my thoughts; I gave them what they asked for.

The next session however, she made no effort to follow through. Was it something I said? Instead, she pointed to DSHS and the DOH, saying they should have taken charge once the study's results were known. They in turn pointed the finger right back. "Only our state Legislature has the authority to mandate automatic testing," said John Peppert, manager of the Department of Health HIV prevention section. "We don't have the authority." I arranged a private meeting with him, but it did no good. He was pleasant enough, but I wasn't looking for pleasantries; I was looking for ownership of the matter. All I got was shifting responsibility. And so it went, back and forth. Why wouldn't anyone step up to the plate? I began feeling as though I was dealing with children, not state agency hierarchy, and elected officials.

Kathy Spears, spokesperson for Children's Services division of DSHS told a reporter, "If exposure to blood-borne pathogens was likely, DSHS would conduct a test. But, if the risk was relatively low,

oftentimes tests weren't done because the procedure hurt the baby." Was she serious? If she thought a blood test "could hurt a baby," what did she think HIV could do to a baby? And what exactly did she mean by, "if exposure was likely?" Ninety-nine percent of my babies fell into the, "likely" category. What did I have to do to hammer it in? The way I saw it, whether the risk was high or low made no difference. If you can save a life, you do.

* * *

While on the Legislative campus I was learning to meet-and-greet, shaking hands instead of shaking in my high heels. That was sorely tested the day I met, then Representative, Jeannie Darneille, 27th district. She became my nemesis. I'd heard rumors concerning her negative response toward my bill, but was totally taken off guard by a chance encounter with her one afternoon outside her office.

She refused to shake my hand, and the first thing out of her mouth was, "This bill will pass over my dead body."

I wasn't prepared for the words she spewed forth, nor did I expect the steely eyes behind the inflection in her voice. I drew back my hand and replied, "In that case, we'll agree to disagree." I knew then what Senator Rockefeller meant, when he said not everyone would agree on the same course of action.

* * *

95

It was 2007. I was almost four years into my battle and still not making much headway. Being just one voice meant it would take more effort on my part to see the resolution I wanted. The pressure was immense. Was I in over my head? The Legislature can seem all-powerful, intimidating, and insurmountable. I reminded myself I'd been in over my head before, and one way or another, things had a way of ending up as they should. The Legislature was, among other things, a building with a dome, bigger than me, yes, but not bigger than my issue.

I made some calls, set up appointments with various legislators, and packed up my babies. I say babies, because they came and went faster than any progress I was making on the bill. Then I headed to my jeweler. Together we designed a diamond encrusted, gold lapel pin with the numbers 3081. Whoever I was meeting with was unlikely to forget the bill number if it was staring them in the face.

Getting to those meetings wasn't always easy with a baby on board, a hundred-and-twenty miles round trip, stopping to change diapers, and fill empty tummies along the way. It was important to put a face on my issue and each baby did that better than I ever could. When I walked through the mall in town, people called me, The Baby Lady. When I walked the marbled corridors of the Legislature, they called me The HIV Lady. Any recognition was better than none, until I met a special someone. To him I meant much more. Newspaper articles covering my story at the time, made me more recognizable in

public. As I sat feeding my baby one afternoon in the mall, a young man, maybe eighteen or nineteen approached and said, "I've read about you, and what you're trying to do. I just wanted to thank you. I

was one of those babies." He was gone in an instant. I didn't get a chance to respond.

When the costly, diamond encrusted, gold numbers failed in my attempt to raise awareness, I went a step further. I went back to my jeweler and asked they make me a gold pin that simply said HIV in bold half-inch letters. My jeweler was stunned. "Mary," she said, "Are you sure you want to wear that?" A week later I picked it up.

It didn't need diamonds to draw attention. I knew it would raise eyebrows, but, even more, I wanted it to raise awareness. I wanted people to ask questions, namely, why do you wear it? Instead they shied away from me, just as they did when I walked my neighbor's rottweiler. To this day, not one person has asked why I wear the pin, and most go out of their way to avoid me. That in itself speaks volumes about what I was up against.

* * *

In early fall that year I read about a Walk For HIV/AIDS in the local newspaper. One hundred people gathered at the waterfront for a two-mile trek through town, in the hope there would soon no longer be a need. Donald and I were front and center carrying a sign covered with a recent newspaper article that high-lighted what I was working on in the legislature. Together, we raised more than twenty thousand dollars, earmarked for services to help those in the county living with HIV/AIDS. That day I was profoundly moved when Natalie Bryson, head of our local HIV/AIDS foundation, recounted something her son James told her before he died from AIDS, "Don't give up the fight five minutes before the miracle." Being part of my community, for something so important inspired me to walk tall with my shoulders back and my head held high.

* * *

If I wasn't on the phone asking for support, I was writing letters, and preparing speeches. I got lots of feedback though not always the kind I wanted, for instance, when I called, the Foster Parent Liaison. I explained what I was fighting for, and asked if she'd support my efforts, speak to other foster parents, and get back to me. She never did. Instead she put a blurb in the Foster Care Association newsletter. It read, "We all need to remember to use precautions when caring for children in our home. We do not know the history of the children, so you should assume they could be carrying any number of diseases. This could include hepatitis and HIV. In your first aid training you were taught how to protect yourself and your family. Please be careful."

She must have felt a cursory caution in the newsletter was sufficient. Had she forgotten the meaning of liaison? The "precautions" she referred to were Universal Precautions which I'd been advised to use time-and-again. The options were endless, as was the list dictating when to use them. By no means do I discredit their effectiveness, but they didn't address the specific needs of the population I dealt with, fragile, four and five pound babies. It was different with them; their bodily fluids came my way, in one form or another, everyday. Any baby, not just those addicted to drugs, can scratch their own face and start a bleed. It's that easy to spread HIV.

To handle each baby as if they were HIV positive would have been a disservice to them. I refused to hold them differently, wear rubber gloves, or don a face shield because they might be HIV positive. They needed to feel my touch, the warmth of my arms, and the beat of my heart when I held them. The blurb in the newsletter kept referring to children. Older children were more apt to take care of their own basic needs, and have an understanding of the importance of personal hygiene. I believed then, as I do now, that early detection is the ultimate life saving measure for babies at high risk. Only then would I use Universal Precautions.

* * *

98

HIV/AIDS is not germane to Africa, as many still believe; it's global, and the ramifications have not lessened when left untreated. In the early 2000's, within walking distance of the White House, the number of infected people was as high as sixty to eighty percent, comparable to the worst areas in Africa. Agencies were patrolling the streets asking the public to get tested. No one can definitively assess the numbers without testing.

* * *

For more than two decades I took my babies to Dr. Susan Reimer, a prominent pediatrician in the community who supported my efforts. She wrote a letter for me to take to the Legislature. Her words were, "Give it to who you feel will act on it, and do what's right for our babies." Because of my babies' life circumstances, she felt it was in their best interest, and reasonable, to adopt policy that would rule out, as well as protect. She believed foster parents had the right to know their potential risks, and thereby better able to undertake the demands of using Universal Precautions. Her letter went unnoticed.

* * *

Always on the lookout for new advances in treatment and management of HIV, my jaw dropped clear to the floor when I read an article written by Kenneth Lovett in the New York Post.

"Babies whose mother's don't get tested for HIV during pregnancy, will automatically be tested within twelve hours of being born so that needed treatment can begin as soon as possible." Health Department spokeswoman Kristine Smith, said, "Babies who receive antiretroviral therapy benefit significantly." The article concluded with, "Mothers who have not already been tested will be urged to do so. If they decline, the babies will be tested without parental consent immediately after birth." Word was spreading, people were talking, and I hoped the article would sway the powers-that-be, in my corner of the world, in my favor.

* * *

I could say I was moving forward here, but I wasn't. Though gathering more support, I was in limbo.

I thought if I did enough research, and got all my ducks-in-a-row, I could persuade Representative Rockefeller to help me again. That didn't happen, he was steadfast in his belief, "I think we arrived at the best we could get." What was I to do now? I couldn't put forth a bill on my own.

A few months went by. I was still caring for sick babies, easing them through withdrawals, all the while feeling sick inside myself. I knew I'd come to the end of the line; I had failed my babies, I had failed myself. The bump in the road was just too big to get around, and when I read about proposed legislation concerning dogs in bars; it was the last straw. Dogs were getting more attention than my babies. It was time to walk away.

> *Dear Editor,*
>
> *"It is with a heavy heart that I put my pen to paper this day to draw to a conclusion my legislative fight of four years; my fight to have drug affected newborns who enter the foster care system tested for HIV. I have written and called everyone I know for help and have been shocked by the general lack of concern in our community.*
>
> *I've met with legislators, talked with a policy analyst, I've met with union organizers, I attended a union summit, I've had front page coverage in the newspaper. I've worked so hard. Four years ago I made a promise to a little girl. I cannot keep that promise. How sad that more importance is placed on dogs in bars.*

It's been ten years since I wrote that letter to the newspaper, one of the hardest things I'd ever done. Today I'm reminded of a quote addressing the dark places courage can lead, but I saw it differently then, I saw it as my lack of courage.

I put it all behind me, for awhile, until I read about Representative Christine Rolfes. She was

hosting a public forum at our community center that afternoon. The article said anyone could speak, address issues they felt needed attention, and get to know our Legislator one-on-one. I must have been well-rested that day, clear headed, and feeling good, because as I leaned over the kitchen sink doing the dishes, I thought, why not? I packed up the baby, and headed into town.

As forty or fifty people gathered outside the center, it soon became clear, no one had a key. I thought, oh, great, I get my courage back and I'm stopped in the parking lot; those bumps in the road were following me.

Someone ran next door to the police station thinking they could help, but short of breaking and entering, there was nothing they could do. An officer hurried over to the nearby Silverdale Hotel, explained the dilemma, and they offered us the use of their conference room. That's how I met Representative Christine Rolfes, a soft spoken, diminutive, middle aged lady who exuded a sense of power and integrity. I knew I was shaking hands with a confident, take charge woman who was ready to go after what she wanted, or, in this case, what I wanted. Little did I know then, a crazy first meeting, outside a locked door, would unlock a decade of indifference based on fear and ignorance. I was back on track for Sue, and all the others.

As the meeting came to order, she asked who'd like to begin. I took a deep breath, raised my hand, and pushed the baby buggy forward, just a little, so she'd see I had a someone with me.

"Perhaps I should go first, since I'm the only one here with a baby, and trust me, when she's had enough, she'll let us know."

Everyone laughed and nodded in agreement. It got the meeting off to a good start, and baby was on her best behavior. When I finished expounding on my issue, we headed to the lobby where Representative Rolfes' aide caught up with us wanting to discuss another meeting in the weeks ahead. It meant she'd taken an interest in what I was trying to accomplish, a fresh start, the turning point I needed to start again.

Once baby was tucked in that evening, I wrote a letter to Representative Rolfes thanking her, and concluded by saying, *"I'm hopeful that some more work on my part, and some intervention on your part, will help my babies who are most at risk, and have the most to lose."*

I didn't realize then just how much work that would involve.

* * *

People needed to know how to make a difference instead of being indifferent. I got in touch with our local Rotary Club president, and asked if I could address their members. I saw no need to beat around the bush. I came right to the point. After discussing my reasons at some length, he said he'd get back with me. Three days later an invitation arrived in the mail. I'd be the guest speaker at their upcoming luncheon.

There was little time to feel nervous, what with everything I already had on my plate. Each evening, after the baby was fast asleep, laundry done, and dishes put away, I was at the dining room table formulating what I was going to say at the luncheon. I wanted to get my point across as effectively as possible, stress the urgency, but not sound whiny or ill-informed. As it turned out I needn't have worried; I was made to feel welcome. My presentation went off without a hitch, and I seemed to stir up a lot of interest. I had high hopes they'd follow through and be supportive.

* * *

Feeling less intimidated with all eyes on me when I spoke, I contacted the Governor's Advisory Council on HIV/AIDS, and arranged a meeting to voice my concerns. They were primarily set up to advise the Governor and Secretary of the Department of Health in developing sound policies. They were also a forum to review and make recommendations about proposed HIV/AIDS related programs and legislation. I wanted to talk to those-in-the-know, and the council members were the people to go to. What I didn't know, was that Representative Darneille was an Ex-Officio member, having the privilege, by virtue of her position, to serve on the board. It wasn't until I was seated in anticipation of addressing the council, that I locked eyes on her. The meeting was called to order.

Having butt heads on more than one occasion over the HIV issue, I'd be lying if I said she didn't make me feel uncomfortable. She was always in the forefront of the line of questioning, but invariably directed her questions to someone else. I wondered if she was doing it deliberately. More often than not, those she questioned replied with,

"I'll have to get back to you on that."

For whatever reasons, we were split in our beliefs, and stubborn in our principles. My goals were bigger than myself and I wasn't going to let her question my integrity, or diminish my confidence.

* * *

I wanted to be on the board of directors of the Kitsap Foster Care Association. If elected, I wouldn't have to rely on anyone but myself to address matters of interest with other foster parents. Their Legislative Liaison position was vacant so I contacted the president, and was invited to attend their next meeting. I told them all about myself, about my ongoing connection with the Legislature, and what I was working on for the foster babies. I was voted in unanimously, then and there. Overjoyed, I felt it was another step in the right direction. I was making myself visible, gathering approval, and getting backing along the way, until a few months down the road.

I was Legislative Liaison just long enough to have two hundred and fifty business cards printed. Board discussions turned to whether or not a board member should be taking part, as opposed to reporting on legislative issues. They didn't ask for my resignation, just made me feel uncomfortable enough that I gave it to them. It read in part,

"I feel strongly the value of every child I hold in my arms, and want to do all I can to make their lives better. It's all encompassing for me and includes participation, involvement, and a certain amount of tenacity. I cannot do that as, just a reporter. I will continue to speak out for every baby, in the hope that one day, they will have strong and effective voices of their own."

I reminded them that they knew what I was working on in the Legislature, my passion, and my steadfastness, the night they voted me into office. It was another bump in the road, but every road has bumps; supposedly they build character. That was one way of looking at it. The position was removed from the board of directors shortly thereafter.

Caring for my babies, as I fought for them, made me even more driven. They were the light at the end of the my tunnel, no matter how rough the road that led me there.

* * *

I had been collaborating with Representative Christine Rolfes regularly since our meeting in the hotel conference room. It was 2008, and she was ready to introduce HB 3119 on my behalf. All my hopes were riding on it, but it was not to be. Seventeen days later, on 02/07/08, it died in committee.

Representative Rolfes said she hadn't realized the bill would be so controversial and a few other legislators were against it as well as Representative Darnielle. Representative Cody however, was outraged that the bill "died," insisting it be brought back the next session, when they'd have more time to fight against political push back. She said we had great success in raising awareness, and pointed out that many more on the committee also wanted testing done.

Christine and I were not to be dissuaded. Now on a first name basis, she explained we'd need to win a ground swell of political support. To have pushed further without it would have created turmoil and interfered with the outcome of other bills on the floor.

My hopes were shattered for the third time. Another bump in the road, but the same promise to the same little girl, remained in the forefront of my mind, and my plans. It was time to bring out the big guns, Bill Gates, Bill Clinton, and Oprah Winfrey.

* * *

Bill Gates is Microsoft co-founder, and head of the Bill and Melinda Gates Foundation. Their primary goal is to support efforts that reduce the global rise in HIV/AIDS. They focus on the poorest countries of Sub-Saharan Africa, and work in conjunction with government agencies, multilateral organizations, academic institutes, and various community organizations. But would they work with, just a Mom, virtually in their own backyard, versus thousands of miles away? I was going to find out.

You'd think by now I'd have some real parchment paper on hand, especially for writing to powerful, influential people, but I didn't. Out came the usual bright yellow legal pad that I so fondly referred to as, faux parchment paper, and started writing. My words were more important than the quality of the paper they were written on. I included a copy of the letter I wrote to Congressman Norm Dicks. It was easier than going into great detail again, and I finished by asking for a letter from Mr. Gates to present to the Legislature in support of HIV testing. Considering we were battling the same monster in the world, and, on the off chance the foundation was very accommodating, I suggested that someone to testify with me would be even better. A week later I received a reply.

> *Dear Mr. and Mrs. Jones,*
>
> *"We have received your letter. Although we appreciate the value of your request, it falls outside our current program guidelines, unfortunately, we will not be able to provide the requested testimony, or a letter of support."*

Perhaps if my return address was somewhere in Africa he would have been more accommodating.

Turns out, Big Gun #1 had no ammunition.

* * *

The next Legislative session was looming. I still needed some hefty help if I was going to make any headway. Unable to sleep one night, I turned on the television. President Clinton and Dr. Sunjay Gupta were on CNN Presents, discussing the worldwide HIV/AIDS epidemic. There was no more sleep for me that night, and by first light I had my pen to paper, again, this time invoking the help of President Clinton. I quoted what I managed to scribble down from both of them during the course of their documentary, which included, "We've let our guard down and need strong prevention policies in place. We need not fear talking about HIV, and we have a moral obligation to do something, whether it's time, money, or SUPPORT. We can

106

make a difference, and because we can ... we must." To which I added my own comment, "Many talk eloquently of how concerned they are about the epidemic, they quote statistics, but I have great difficulty getting them to put their pens where their mouths are."

In the days following I received a reply. Always more than eager to be of assistance, the Postmaster started giving me odd looks when I picked up my mail. I think he was impressed with the caliber of my more recent pen pals. The letter read,

Dear Ms. Jones,

"On behalf of President Clinton, thank you for requesting his endorsement for mandatory HIV/AIDS testing of foster children. I regret that the former President is unable to provide such an endorsement. He would want to be closely involved in any project to which he lends his support or name, and his current set of obligations does not allow him to devote the necessary amount of time to this endeavor."

How much time would a letter have taken from his busy schedule?

President Clinton founded The Clinton Health Initiative to help save the lives of millions living with HIV/AIDS in the developing world. They believe that well-timed, targeted interventions can dramatically reduce mortality. How is it then, when I asked for his help, to do just that, in his own part of the world, he had no time? Nor could I believe that the battle for my babies' health and well being, for their very lives, no less, was referred to as an "endeavor." What happened to the, "Moral obligation to do something, whether it be time, money, or SUPPORT ?" All I asked for was a letter; maybe I should have enclosed a stamp.

Big Gun #2 turned out to be nothing more than a squirt gun.

* * *

Though my babies kept a smile on my face, inside I was tormented and angry with the highfalutin society I was living in. People seeming, or trying to seem, great and important, all the while missing the mark.

On my next trip to the Capitol, a dear friend called me into her office having noticed, in her words, my "lackluster appearance, instead of my usual enthusiasm and vitality." She handed me a note that said, Mary, you are doing great things. I know it doesn't feel like it all the time, with such overwhelming bureaucracy to deal with, but, if enough people like you keep speaking up, things will change.

It was better than a hug, and just what I needed to hear. It took my focus off, woe is me, and turned it back in the right direction, my promise.

* * *

I know this will sound like the fateful intervention of supernatural influences, but over the course of the many years I worked on this legislation, three times I was awakened during the night and found something concerning HIV on television, without even turning the channels. It was as if I was meant to tune in.

The first time was when HB 3081 was being debated on the floor of the House. I was half asleep when I realized; they're discussing my bill! I sat bolt upright.

A few years later, I awoke again in the wee hours, turned on the television to find President Clinton, and Doctor Sunjay Gupta exchanging thoughts on the HIV epidemic. But it wasn't until the third time that I started to think it was really uncanny.

At 2:30 a.m. I awoke, turned the television on yet again, and as before, without changing channels, there was Oprah Winfrey, at an orphanage in South Africa. Christened, God 's Golden Acre,

volunteers brought healing and hope to AIDS orphans. Loss, and desperation underscored the features of their tiny faces, too young to fully comprehend the enormity of their situation.

Oprah was there to make a donation and a documentary giving God's Golden Acre a profile for the world to see, including me, in the darkness of my bedroom, when, for whatever reason, I just happened to tune in early that morning.

True to form, hours later out came my faux parchment paper, and with pen in hand, I started writing. This time I didn't ask for anything, not even a letter.

I told her who I was, and what I was doing for my babies. I wanted her to know I cared.

"I am one person, one voice, but I can do a lot; I can change a law. It may not have global ramifications, but it's a start. As you alluded to in the documentary, I too pray that it will raise consciousness in my part of the world. I feel we are working toward the same end, and together, we are two voices."

I checked the mail everyday for weeks but got no response.

Big Gun #3 miss-fired.

* * *

How many times would I have to start over in my journey, how many defeats before I'd see the results I was hoping for. Sometimes I felt I was all alone taking on the world. How could I ever have presumed to make a difference on such a massive scale? Was I part of the same highfalutin society that I railed against? Did I have my priorities in the right place, and why-oh-why was change so hard?

An article in the newspaper jumped out at me one day as I was having lunch at the Capitol in Olympia. It set me straight in short order. It was about President Abraham Lincoln, how he led the country through the most difficult period in history. Listed were the many failures and obstacles he faced and overcame before becoming the leader of our nation. The article asked readers, *to think of setbacks you have faced in your own life, and how you responded. Lincoln may have failed many times, but somehow he always failed upward. He was propelled by a sense of mission, and he was willing and able to do whatever it took to get that great mission accomplished.

It was impossible to read that and not feel compelled to realign, suck it up, and find another way, a better way.

* * *

That was easier said than done. When you're dealing with the Legislature, there aren't countless ways to bring about change. There are, however, many legislators you can approach and, if you're lucky, everyone comes together, there's a meeting of minds, and bills are passed, effecting change. When all seemed hopeless, as it had many times, I relied on sheer determination and inner strength to strategize and keep moving forward, one step at a time.

* * *

Representative Rolfes suggested I get some input from the local HIV/AIDS foundation. I called and set up a date and time to address their next board of directors meeting. I wasn't too sure how they'd perceive me, though I was quite sure they'd heard about me. I wondered if that was good or bad. In any case, by now I'd learned, if you had the guts to open your mouth, you'd better be responsible for what came out. Turns out I was received warmly, we talked, they listened, then asked what they could do to help. I was quick to respond with, "How about one of you testifying with me for my upcoming bill?" They agreed.

More and more people were talking about HIV; that was essential if mindsets were ever going to change. The complacency and fear I'd confronted when I first got involved was diminishing. Though it was encouraging, there was still a long way to go.

* * *

House Bill 1046 was introduced and read for the first time on January 12, 2009. Yet again my hopes were riding on this one. The language was much the same as the others, interspersed with the usual, act relating to, referred to Committee, pursuant to, in as much as, or, as otherwise expressed. Politics tends to have a language of its own and can be a little off-putting at first. Still, I knew I had to be patient. It didn't help when the day after it was introduced, the Governor's Advisory Council on HIV/AIDS decided not to take a position on the bill at this time. I wasn't at the meeting, but Representative Darneille was.

On January 20, 2009, the bill had a public hearing. As I'd done for each one prior, I was there to testify in favor. So was someone from Lifelong AIDS in Seattle, but, as they'd also done for each one before, they testified against it. To make matters worse, no one from my local HIV/AIDS foundation showed up to testify as they'd promised. Instead, they called the day before the hearing to say they wouldn't be able to participate. Was there a connection between their last minute change of heart, the Council's tenuous position, and the continued presence of Representative Darneille at my every turn in the road? Determination wasn't going to be enough this time, but my purpose was strong as ever.

* * *

The state budget was being debated that session, facing an eight million dollar shortfall, and Governor Gregoire was considering vast cuts in state spending. Then came the bomb shell, a fiscal note was attached to my bill, the death knell.

A fiscal note provides legislators with relevant and time sensitive data that is accessible and actionable. It delivers predictive analytics of proposed government action to determine its impact. In simple terms, testing the babies was too expensive. The Department of Health estimated it would cost about $500,000.00 a year. It could be argued that it would save the state money in the long run, by preventing HIV/AIDS related health care costs throughout the life of a foster child, but because of the state's mounting financial problems, it didn't look good. That seemed to be a recurring theme for me. I knew then and there it was the end of the line for HB 1046.

* * *

It wasn't long after when three-day old Anthony arrived. In a letter to Representative Rolfes discussing our next plan of action, I made mention of the new man in my life, hoping to change the mood and end on a lighter note. "He's only a few days old, cute as can be, doesn't talk back, and is agreeable to go wherever I want, when I want. I can overlook messy diapers and spit up." She replied, "I always look forward to your letters because even in defeat and great disappointment, you manage to take the stiffness out of politics." I took that as a compliment.

* * *

If stress levels are a good predictor of the color of your hair, let me just say, mine skipped gray and went straight to snow white. The only time I wasn't stressed was when I was caring for the babies; my issues paled in comparison. When you watch a newborn struggle to survive, you see what real strength

112

looks like; you hear it in their screams; you feel it in their violent withdrawal seizures. But most of all, you digest it when you look into their eyes and know you are all they have in the world.

* * *

That September I received a letter from Representative Rolfes' legislative assistant, Sarah. The Governor's Advisory Council had drafted a letter to the Governor with their recommendations concerning the CDC's position on HIV testing. I was asked to read it over and get back to her with my thoughts on the matter. I appreciated the fact that my opinions were valued.

Sarah,

As I read the letter to the Governor, a couple of things came to mind. The reference to routine, and screening, have me in a quandary; are they the same as mandatory and testing? If they are one and the same, great care has been taken not to use the words mandatory and testing.

The way I see it, The Advisory Council is saying the CDC's recommendations for testing are going to happen sooner or later. So Sarah, lets get on board; why is Washington State dragging it's feet? When I had House Bill 3119 introduced, I asked that our state be in the forefront, as were five other states at the time. Why doesn't anyone ever listen to me?(ha ha) If the Governor signs on to the CDC's plan for this state, I must ask, why not the entire population? If enacted here, it will be a step forward, all will benefit from, screening or testing, and if it's routine or mandatory for everyone, no one can complain about stereotyping.

It would be seven years before someone did listen.

* * *

113

I researched the Elizabeth Glazer Pediatric AIDS Foundation in Washington D.C. Their name alone filled me with renewed hope of getting legislation passed.

Elizabeth Glazer contracted the AIDS virus through a blood transfusion in 1981 while giving birth. It was later learned she passed the virus on to her daughter through breast milk, and a few years later, to her son in utero. She and two close friends created the foundation with one critical mission: to bring hope to children with AIDS. Few researchers were focusing on issues specific to the need, there were no drugs available for children, and at the time, the infection rate was increasing. The foundation set out to change all that. They were dedicated to preventing pediatric HIV infection and eradicating pediatric AIDS through research, advocacy, prevention, and treatment programs. They were also instrumental in making sure in every area of the Federal government, from research priorities at the National Institutes of Health, to the halls of Congress, children with HIV were no longer forgotten.

I couldn't put my pen to paper fast enough. After explaining who I was and what I was up against, I got right down to business.

"I need the support and backing of an organization such as yours if I'm ever to get a bill passed

into law. My last foster baby came into this world in critical condition, weighed just over a

a pound and addicted to drugs. When I brought her home I could see and feel the shunt in her

brain. I could see the scar from her heart surgery. I tripped over hundreds of feet of oxygen

tubing throughout my house. I ran to her side every time her heart monitor alarmed to make sure

114

she started breathing again. I could hear her chronic lung disease. But, I couldn't see if she had HIV."

The state spent hundreds of thousands of dollars to keep her alive before I brought her home, then sent her out into the world not knowing if she'd still be alive ten or fifteen years later without a simple, inexpensive test and six weeks of treatment." I concluded with, "I will be back at the Capitol next year, but I'll need more than my own voice. Please let me know your thoughts and ideas. They replied,

"We were all very moved by your words and your life's work of caring for so many children. The issue of testing infants in foster care for HIV/AIDS falls OUTSIDE the scope of the Foundation's work. Our Public Policy staff has contacted the Congressional Coalition on Adoption Institute, (CCAI), who specialize in working with Congress on foster care and adoption matters. Their office will contact you with further input concerning the issues you have brought to our attention."

They thanked me for contacting their foundation, then added insult to injury by saying,

"We wish you all the best in your efforts on behalf of children."

The foundation that I'd put the most hope in, passed the buck. Though they had expanded their focus to battle the pandemic around the globe, it didn't include foster babies at high risk for infection... in Washington State. I was outside someone else's scope, again. What would it take to get inside? CCAI, in turn, enlisted the help of U.S.Congressman Jim McDermott to review my letter. In the weeks following I received their collective opinions in the mail.

After researching your issues, by our office, and Congressman McDermott's office, it has come to our attention that, because there is very minimal risk of HIV transmission, and due to concerns

of both privacy and high costs associated with testing, it would not be in the State's best

interest to preform mandatory HIV tests on these infants.

The letter went on to further describe more of what they based their conclusions on.

We appreciate your concerns and are certainly sympathetic to them and the barriers you have

faced promoting this legislation: however, based on our understanding, the lack of this

mandatory testing has not resulted in any harm to either foster parents or children, and is not a

significant public safety concern.

How would they know? No one was testing. I took it in the gut again.

I did some further research regarding Congressman McDermott's stance on the

HIV/AIDS epidemic. Only a year earlier, in July 2008, he was speaking out in strong support of HR 5501 saying,

America stands with commitment, compassion, and conviction against the HIV/AIDS pandemic.

Everyday more than a thousand children around the world are born infected. We know that providing a short regimen of antiretroviral drugs to the mother and newborn reduces

transmission rates by fifty percent. Let us stand together as one nation and one world, united in

one common goal in the fight against HIV/AIDS.

He may have professed to be in favor of "standing together," but clearly I was standing alone. It felt as though everyone were opening their mouths, but more often than not, all that came out was rhetoric, lacking in sincerity, and little, if any, meaningful content. One nation, one world he said, united in one goal. I guess I fell way short of a nation, much less the world. I cried, asking myself over and over, what's it going to take?

* * *

Election years were another hurtle to get over. No one wanted to take on controversial bills. If it

wasn't one thing, it was another, but I dug my feet in and kept putting one in front of the other, reminding myself, "If it's worth having, it's worth fighting for." I had five bills under my belt by now, except for one, they were introduced in consecutive sessions with various amendments. At this rate, the babies I was fighting for would soon be young adults... if they were among the lucky ones.

* * *

It was 2013. Even though we had a series of failed attempts behind us, now Senator Rolfes and I were ready to try again, spurred on by the latest arrival in my life.

A baby girl addicted to drugs, spent her first months of life in a Pediatric Interim Care Center to ensure medical oversight and a successful and safe placement as soon as possible. She had to be on a morphine regimen to come off the myriad of illegal controlled substances her tiny body absorbed while still in utero, then weened off the morphine. Babies like her don't just go through addiction withdrawals, they suffer through.

As I prepared to bring her home, I asked, and kept asking to have her tested for the HIV virus. No one listened. More months went by. Though I had a request for the blood work from her pediatrician, I still couldn't get the court order to have it done. I went up the chain of command at DSHS. I went to supervisors, I met with regional and area administrators. I went through countless pads of faux parchment paper, writing letter after letter, to anyone, and everyone I thought could help, it was all in vain.

I was sixty-four, tired, and now needed more naps than my babies. Common sense dictated I could no longer care for them, while at the same time traverse the many miles back and forth to the Capitol fighting for them. I was so fed up with the "system," frustrated, and worn down, that I closed my license. I was no longer a foster mother.

Within days my world, as I'd known it for so long, came crashing down around me, replaced with stillness, emptiness, and incredible silence. The two cribs, where toothless smiles once peered through the rails, now stood empty.

* * *

"Guardian Angel to Fragile Babies. Advocate, foster mom, leaves legacy after thirty-one years," read the headline on the front page of the Kitsap Sun on January 20, 2013. My love for the babies came down to those fourteen words, over the course of a lifetime. It said I left a legacy. Had I died? I still had unfinished business, and no intention of going anywhere until I'd kept my promise.

The article called me "a squeaky wheel," said, "my passion for the babies was unrelenting, that I

was determined, and persistent." But I wasn't the Energizer Bunny anymore, I felt more like a hamster running in circles. I was overwhelmed and flattered by the newspaper article and basked in the limelight for several days. Then it was time to get down to business, again. The only thing that had changed was, now I had the eyes of the entire community watching. Talk about pressure.

* * *

Adjusting to anything can be hard. The babies defined "me" for so long I'd forgotten who I was before diapers, bibs, and "The Little Engine That Could." Over time I found my own special meaning in that little engine. If it could, so could I.

There would be no more babies in my home, in my life, or in my arms. I began to question the decision to close my license. Was it made in haste, was I thinking of myself and not the babies? I retreated to a place within where I thought I wouldn't feel the loss, the pain, and the regret. I immersed my energy in volunteer work with the Red Cross. I became a licensed Parent Partner with Kitsap Mental Health. I took a seat on the board of the YWCA. But nothing filled the void. I couldn't pass the nurseries without walking in and remembering their little faces, counting their tiny toes, and humming my favorite lullabies. I'd often sit in the rocker, as I'd done time and again, and remember the feel of their warm breath against my cheek.

Eight months after the last baby left, I closed the nursery doors as well as that part of my life. It took me that long to let go. I'd come to terms with the ending and knew I had done the right thing. It was time to move on with renewed purpose. My babies no longer needed me to change their diapers. They needed me to change laws.

* * *

I was preparing to testify again, this time for Senate Bill 5454 and enlisted the help of Big Gun #4,

my dear friend, and foster mother, Judith Lockridge. I figured if one of us was a force to be

reckoned with, imagine the power of two.

I had addressed several Foster Parent meetings over the course of my struggle for legislation, and asked if they were concerned about the HIV issue surrounding children in their care; they said yes. The power of two should have been the power of hundreds on the steps of the Legislature, speaking out and changing the course of subsequent rulings. But only Judy stepped up to the plate.

With the calm of a seasoned professional speaker, Judy scanned the room and began her testimony for SB 5454. She had their attention right from the start, didn't mince words, and got to the heart of the matter. "My name is Judith Lockridge. As a Foster parent and Adoptive parent, I have had several newborns in my care. Most all the babies have been drug affected and have not received prenatal care. All children placed in out of home care have special needs. As a Foster parent, I am charged with, and able to address these needs. I have spent hours, sometimes days, in doctors offices and hospitals hoping to enable the child to be the best they can. Does a child, born in the United States, not have the right to be treated if their life is threatened by HIV or Hepatitis, through no fault of their own? Please, we must know, we must test."

Big Gun #4 was well spoken and powerful. Gates, Clinton and Winfrey could have learned a thing or two from her.

Then it was my turn. Eye to eye with committee members, I settled into my chair, pulled the microphone toward me, then froze momentarily. Senator Darneille was sitting off to my left.

Among the things I repeated in my testimonies over the years, I told those assembled before me how my last baby, had already gone through hell and back. If she does have HIV, she may have to go through hell again, and might not come back. I told them, she had a right to the best medical care available. Had I concerns about any other health related issue, a referral from her pediatrician would have been sufficient to warrant treatment. Each day DSHS waited put her life at greater risk. I went on, every child deserves a lifetime.

They weren't prepared for a question, least of all from me, when I asked, "Who should she go to, in the years ahead, if she is HIV positive, and ask, why didn't you care enough to save my life?"

The room echoed deafening silence. I wasn't done. I went on to tell them about the day she left my home, when I asked the social worker, if and when the state had her tested, could I get the results should I need testing and treatment myself. I got a resounding, no.

There have been a few times in my life when I've been so angered I thought I'd explode, this was one of those times. They told me that since I'd closed my license, and was no longer a foster parent, confidential test results would not be shared with me. They couldn't have cared less about my health risk, I could only hope they cared more about the babies'.

I was pushing the time limit allowed to deliver my testimony, but unless someone told me to shut up and sit down, I wasn't stopping. Would they dare try to quiet "The Little Engine That Could?" I ended with this afterthought just as the Chair of the Committee began to squirm in his seat. "I believe there could be children in the foster care system who are HIV positive and adopted into families who don't know."

Senate Bill 5454 didn't make it through session that year having been passed from pillar-to-post eighteen times. At the request of Seattle's HIV/AIDS Alliance, it was placed on hold in hopes of passing broader legislation in 2016, making sure there would be no barriers for babies or children to be tested. It would also ensure court orders were more attainable upon request.

I was never privy to the reason behind Senator Darneille's stand against HIV testing other than the fact she served as Executive Director of the Pierce County AIDS Foundation from 1989 to 2007, a time when HIV/AIDS was viewed very differently. When we first met, she told me my bill would pass over her dead body. So it came right out of left field when she did a complete turn around and became the prime sponsor of my next bill.

* * *

Senate Bill 5728 was introduced in the legislature on January 30, 2015 and referred to the Health Care Committee. A public hearing was held on February 10th, and another on February 25th, in the Senate Committee on Ways and Means. I wasn't apprised of either one, a communication mix-up I was told. Instead, a powerful trio, who had opposed testing for as long as I'd fought for it, showed up to testify in favor, including Senator Darneille, the prime sponsor, a representative from Lifelong AIDS Alliance in Seattle, and a representative from the Washington State Department of Health. The sudden change of interest and direction worried me. In the end, their approach seemed to work out for the best, opening doors that had other-wise been bolted during my thirteen year tenure walking the halls of the legislature. But it was still just a plan, seeing it through to fruition was a leap of faith, or so I thought. Two days later, on February 27th it was voted do pass as Substitute Senate Bill 5728 in the Senate Committee on Ways and Means. Throughout the three consecutive Special Sessions that year, it was "reintroduced and retained in present status" until January 11, 2016, the start of the next Regular Session, when it was brought forward for the fifth time.

Senator Darneille, still wanted nothing to do with me. This time I relied on myself to track all movement on the bill and on February 23, 2016, took my seat in front of the microphone to testify, with a certain amount of trepidation.

"The HIV virus has not gone away, and neither have I." I went on to say, since I'd first brought my issue to their attention, advances in medical intervention were remarkable and life saving, but Washington State needed to go further in it's approach to meeting the need. I explained how, if bundled together with standard prenatal tests, HIV screening would be more accepted and become standard practice, an approach already proven successful in other states. In summation I told them I had retired, but as an advocate for all babies, I would keep on speaking out, "Many people listen," I said, "My new job is to get them to hear." I asked they vote yes in support of Substitute Senate Bill 5728.

On March 7, 2016 the Senate concurred with House amendments.

On March 8th , the President of the Senate signed in favor.

On March 9th , the Speaker of the House signed in favor.

On March 29th, myself, Senator Rolfes, and Senator Darneille stood beside Governor Inslee as he

signed my bill into law.

* * *

Considering all the twists and turns in the road leading up to that day, the last turn moved me to tears for a couple of reasons. After Governor Inslee signed the official papers, he handed the pen to Senator Darneille who said, "Mary deserves this more than me" and placed it in my hand. It was a defining moment.

I felt the real victory had been snatched from our grasp when Senator Darneille, now the prime sponsor, swept in and took the credit, overshadowing the years of work Senator Rolfes and I had put into it. I was happy the bill passed, it was a huge step forward in the fight against HIV, but I wasn't happy with the circumstances surrounding the finish line.

As I stood before a bank of photographers, smiling and shaking hands with Governor Inslee, I had but one thought on my mind, setting up a meeting with Lifelong AIDS Alliance. It was salient to everything I'd worked for, everything I stood for, and my promise to a baby girl. It wasn't over yet.

There was a lot I didn't understand, but I intended to find out. It infuriated me that Senator Darneille's platform was almost a carbon copy of what I'd been telling the Legislature for thirteen years. "My" bill had been signed into law, but it didn't feel like mine anymore. I chewed up my feelings, swallowed my pride and went looking for answers. I wasn't seeing the language that addressed what I'd been hoping for, the population I was fighting for, the twelve hour time frame, and proof of prompt access to court orders. The bill required all pregnant women to be screened for the virus, but where did that leave the babies if their mother opted out, refusing to be tested?

* * *

"HIV Bill Means More Tests" My fight made the front page of the Kitsap Sun, again, in 2016, though this time in smaller print, and relegated off to the side. "Tracyton woman key to legislation. Mary Jones won the war, but her battle continues." It went on to say, "Mary was really a hero in getting this passed," but when I read the next sentence my heart sank. It was what I feared most, and it was the first time anyone came right out and said, "babies under the state's care weren't included in the law."

The newspaper quoted what I'd said all along. "My moms wake up under bridges, in the woods and in doorways. Most of them get no prenatal care. The first time they see a doctor is when the baby is being born." The article concluded with Senator Rolfes promising to talk to DSHS in an attempt to take another look at my issues.

I couldn't wrap my brain around all that had transpired. Ages fifteen to sixty-five and all pregnant women would now be tested. But what about innocent newborns, they had no voice, and now they had no rights.

* * *

Looking back over my many years as a foster mother, I saw myself simply as a mother. I'd have done anything for my babies, as would any parent, so when baby Sue left in 2003 with her forever family, I resigned to be her voice and do everything I could to correct a wrong. It was nearing the end of 2017 when Senator Rolfes agreed to help, yet again, to make that happen.

Senate Bill 6580 was introduced in the legislature on January 30th 2018. From that day forward my phone was never out of my sight as countless times, from early morning to the last thing every night, I checked on the bill's progression. It is said, "the wheels of justice turn slowly." I was finding out, the wheels of legislation weren't much faster. Initially, I thought all I had to do was ask nicely and use the word please. That wasn't working.

It was a stressful time for everyone, not just me. Hillary Clinton lost her presidential bid to become the first female president of the United States, North Korea continued launching nuclear tests over the Pacific Ocean, a series of natural disasters including hurricanes, earthquakes, and devastating fires, made headline news around the globe, and in Small Town, USA, I was still grappling for legislation to help the babies.

I went down to the legislature to testify. I never tired of the feelings I got when I was at the Capitol. Seeing the dome in all its glory, walking the impressive marbled hallways, and looking down from galleries to the chambers below where laws were made. It was there I felt the enormity of what I was trying to accomplish, empowering, though at times scary and intimidating.

* * *

This time when I introduced myself, the Chair of the public hearing remarked, "I remember you!" I wondered if that was a good or bad sign. Were they growing tired of seeing me, hearing me say the same things? Every time I testified I was reminded of my babies and their mothers who exposed them to life threatening conditions, depriving them of the chance for a healthy life. I was going to keep saying the same things, over and over, as many times as I had to until they listened. I reached for the microphone.

"Madam Chair, members of the committee, when you have walked in my shoes there can be no doubt how important this bill is. It makes early detection of HIV possible, the ultimate life-saving measure. We can end AIDS in Washington State and this bill is a step in the right direction. If we stand tall together we can make it happen. I strongly support SB 6580."

* * *

My fight had been long and hard, a constant roller-coaster ride of emotions, but on March 6th 2018, my bill was delivered to the Governor's desk. I'm sure in the days following, Senator Rolfes and her assistant grew weary of my numerous emails inquiring if there was a date for the signing yet. Always in the back of my mind was the possibility the Governor could veto the entire bill, or parts of it. Fortunately, that didn't happen and it was subsequently signed into law on March 21, 2018 with me, Senator Rolfes, and Senator Darneille proudly standing at his side.

Just getting to his office was a major feat in-and-of itself. Hundreds of bill signing participants lined the hallway, as an aid screamed, at the top of his lungs, the number of each bill in line to be signed. It added to the build-up and excitement. Several people whose paths I had crossed in my determination to get to this day came up to shake my hand, give me a hug, and congratulate me. I was caught up in it all, still not believing it was really happening.

It had taken fifteen years, but at long last I kept my promise. Henceforth, HIV testing would require the same notification and consent requirement as any other medical test.

* * *

The days leading up to the signing can best be described as taxing, frustrating, intense, and nerve-wracking, as I waited in anticipation, all of which culminated with a smile, a handshake, and a signature, at most lasting two minutes, after a span of nearly 6,000 days in the making.

It was a heart pounding moment, but one of the best in my lifetime. The wrong had finally been made right.

When all was said and done, some might wonder if I partied the night away in celebration. Rather, I went home, washed my face, and crawled into bed. The release of pressure was immense; I was exhausted, and didn't know if I should laugh or cry. Instead, I went to sleep.

The next morning a reporter and photographer showed up at my door bright and early, and a few days thereafter, my fight for the babies made headline news again. This time it felt like a victory lap. It was over.

I did the leg work; at times I had to shout; but when the law makers finally listened; it was Sue's voice they heard, not mine.

Endnote

Over the course of the fifteen long years I fought for legislation, it wasn't until it became law that I realized it wasn't really "My bill" after all.

There were three strong women in the arena; we just didn't know in the beginning it would take action on the part of all three to reach the desired conclusion.

Granted, I started the ball rolling, and kept it rolling. I was persistent and determined, but without Senator Rolfes and Senator Darneille's help, it would never have come to fruition, proving

*There is strength in numbers, yes, but even more so in collective good will. For those endeavors are supported by mighty forces unseen.

*Richelle E. Goodrich

Newspaper Articles

The following pages show newspaper articles that were published about Mary's work as a foster mother and her achievements in the legislation of the Washington State foster care system.

Fig. 1: March 2018, Triumph in HIV Bill

The Seattle Times

LOCALNews

seattletimes.com/localnews | AUGUST 10, 2008 | SUNDAY

THE SEATTLE TIMES AND SEATTLE POST-INTELLIGENCER

Foster-care system still struggling

CHILDREN'S ADMINISTRATION

State agency has not yet fulfilled '04 Braam settlement, but governor says safety of all children is a high priority

BY MAUREEN O'HAGAN
Seattle Times staff reporter

A month ago, a Whatcom County jury told the state Children's Administration to quit complaining and start acting.

"You need to go do whatever it takes," Superior Court Judge Charles

PHOTOS BY RYAN BRENNAN / THE SEATTLE TIMES

Seattle officer held in Sturgis shooting

HELLS ANGELS MEMBER WOUNDED

Confrontation erupts at South Dakota event

BY JIM BROADER
Seattle Times staff reporter

Pigments of imagination

ABOVE: Six-month-old Oliver Brown is cradled in the arms of his father, Craig, a tattoo artist from Tacoma, on Saturday at the seventh South Tattoo Expo at Seattle Center. Oliver was born into a tattoo world. **RIGHT:** Rudy Cisneros, from Orange County, Calif., shows off images of actresses Marta Pelle, left, Marilyn Monroe and Lupe Velez. The artist is her husband, Rudy Cisneros. The expo continues noon-10 p.m. today with music, contests, exhibits, seminars and on-site tattooing. Admission, $15. Info: www.seattlecentertapexpo.org.

How to share the road

Answering readers' questions about cycling and driving

Q Why don't cyclists have to be licensed?

A

COMING MONDAY IN THE SEATTLE TIMES: Answers to readers' top questions about the rules of the road

WEB EXTRA
More answers to reader questions: seattletimes.com/localnews

GOP claims Gregoire backs state income tax: Does she?

ELECTIONS 08

This is the first in an occasional series of stories truth-squadding campaign ads, mailers and candidate statements.

BY RACHEL THOMAS
Seattle Times Olympia bureau

OLYMPIA — It's an interesting positive bound to lose of its before the November election that Democratic Gov. Chris Gregoire is in favor of adopting a state income tax.

Is it true?

It all depends on how the claim is framed. Gregoire has suggested she thinks an income tax is a good idea and that one eventually will become reality in Washington. But she also has said repeatedly that now is not the time and she has no intention of pushing for one.

Republican Dino Rossi and the state GOP recently put out fliers that blast Gregoire for sharply increasing state spending since she took office in 2005.

Rossi's flier, which is being handed out door to door and at campaign events, also states flatly that Gregoire supports state income tax. The Republican Party flier is...

Truth check

THE CLAIM

THE FACTS

OUR RULING

HALF TRUE

DAVID COOPER / THE SEATTLE TIMES

Fig. 2: August 2008, Foster-care System Sruggling

Fig. 3: August 2008, Foster-care System Still Sruggling cont.

Mary Jones cares for a 5-month-old baby in November at her home in Trabyton. After more than three decades fostering infants and children — many born to drug- or alcohol-addicted mothers — Jones is retiring from foster care.

Guardian ANGEL to fragile BABIES

Jones gets a hug from Ch'laya, one of her former foster children. When Ch'laya was born, she had myriad medical needs. Today, "she's just a normal little girl, doing these normal things," Jones said.

■ Advocate, foster mom leaves legacy after 31 years

By Brynn Grimley
bgrimley@kitsapsun.com
360-792-9249

TRACYTON — Peering from the fur-lined hood of her down jacket, 4-year-old Ch'laya Roberts begged her mom to let her stay with "Mama Mary."

Six-year-old twin siblings A'niya and Amani chimed in, pleading for the chance to sleep over.

Their mother, Shawntel Roberts, turned to Mary Jones and teased she'd be more than happy to leave her hyperactive brood behind in exchange for some peace and quiet.

Jones, who fostered Ch'laya as an infant before Roberts adopted her, assured the children she'd see them again soon.

As the family left and stillness returned to her two-story Central Kitsap home, Jones, 63, beamed as she reflected on the evening's theatrics — Ch'laya and A'niya performing dance routines and Amani singing his ABCs.

Four years ago, Jones cared for Ch'laya — a baby born premature to a drug-addicted mother. At one point, Ch'laya was connected to an oxygen machine and had to have surgery to place a shunt in her brain. Another surgery fixed her heart.

To hear Ch'laya and her siblings scream and giggle now is Jones' reward at the end of a 31-year career as a foster mother. During 15 of those years, she cared for the state's most fragile babies, many born to alcohol- and drug-addicted mothers.

See JONES, 4A

■ INSIDE Former foster mom Mary Jones hopes HIV-testing bill for babies, which she's been fighting for since 2004, becomes law. 5A

Fig. 4: January 2013, Guardian Angel to Frigile Babies

Fig. 5: Area Foster Mother Pushes for Protection

Thank you, Jesus!

Thank you, Jesus is what I want to say,
On this Your special holy birthday.

You know my story and how I got my start,
How birth mom and I have always been apart.

You saved me from a life that looked dark and quite scary,
And placed me in the care of a sweet lady named Mary.

On eighteen balloons, Mary let me fly,
And I drifted up higher into the sky.

I was scared and confused and thought it wouldn't stop,
Then into the arms of an angel, you let me drop.

I wasn't sure she was an angel, but her face was just glowing
While out of her heart, pure love kept on flowing.

I haven't known many angels, as you might have guessed,
But it seems the one you gave me must be the best.

She packs me around, then sings me a song,
And gives me gogurt and bapes all the day long.

When I hear her voice, I take off like a rocket,
And I never go night night without a passy and cocket.

You say she's not an angel, then what could she be,
For she spends all her time concerned about me?

I've already got an angel, is that what you said!
So you decided to give me something better instead.

You could have given me an angel named Gabriel or Tommy,
But you went one step further and gave me a Mommy.

Now I thank you, Jesus, for I have reason to boast,
Because you gave me the Mommy, I needed the most.

MJB